You Are **POWERFUL**

How to Overcome It All and Take Back Your Power

SAM KNIGHT

Licensed Alcohol and Drug Counselor
Psychotherapist, Life Coach and Motivational Speaker

Copyright 2022 Sukimo Knight

All rights reserved. No part of this publication may be reproduced, distributed, or transmitted in any form or by any means, including photocopying, recording, or other electronic or mechanical methods, without the prior written permission of the publisher, except in the case of brief quotations embodied in critical reviews and certain other noncommercial uses permitted by copyright law. For permission requests, write to the publisher.

ISBN: 979-8-9868322-0-3 (Paperback)
ISBN: 979-8-9868322-1-0 (eBook)
Library of Congress Control Number: 2022915699

Published by Dara Publishing, LLC
Cover and Book design by Kamaljeet Singh
Printed in the United States of America.

Disclaimer: The publisher and the authors do not make any guarantee or other promise as to any results that may be obtained from using the content of this book. This publication is meant as a source of valuable information for the reader, however it is not meant as a substitute for direct expert assistance. If such level of assistance is required, the services of a competent professional should be sought.

Dedication

May you always remember that you are powerful- Ladybug, Baby Allen, and Valli.

To my brother who was murdered by the police in 2006, Antonio "Tony" Bryant, may your story live on forever.

To every client I have ever served, I hope you never forget how powerful you are.

Table Of Contents

Foreword by Dr. Judith James, Ed. D, MA, LADC

Introduction

Author's Note

Chapter 1 - Childhood Sexual Abuse — 17

Chapter 2 - Generational Cycles — 25

Chapter 3 - The Power of Addiction — 33

Chapter 4 - Abandonment — 43

Chapter 5 - The Mindset of hopelessness — 55

Chapter 6 - Acceptance — 63

Chapter 7 - Shame and Guilt — 71

Chapter 8 - Lost and Found — 85

Chapter 9 - The Power of a Man — 99

Chapter 10 - Breakthrough — 113

Chapter 11 - You are Powerful — 121

About the Author

Acknowledgment

Foreword

I started working in addiction recovery at a later point in my life. Prior to that, I had been a teacher and coach. While working on my degree, my course work in Alcohol and Drug Addiction Counseling came from academic books, articles, and essays. Although these resources offered an important perspective into the field, they could not capture the essence of the stories present in the addiction field

Then, at my third treatment center, I met Sam. I was impressed with her ability to stay calm among large groups of people who had achieved only a few weeks of sobriety. I was also astonished by her creativity in facilitating client groups, and the serenity she naturally brought into a room. After reading *You are Powerful*, I saw that my first impressions of her made sense. She is a woman whose light was too bright to ever extinguish and now she has shared it with us in this book.

Sam's story reflects sacrifice, survival, and wisdom. In *You are Powerful*, she creates imagery, evokes emotion, and captivates her readers as she describes the trauma she endured as a child. She includes the barriers she faced, her unique circumstances, and her resistance to giving up all while demonstrating how she powered through a plethora of obstacles. In her story, Sam draws a complex map of someone who's met incredible disappointment head-on and turned it into profound insight. Sam's resistance to becoming satisfied with others' assumptions about her is evident throughout her story.

There is an accumulative effect while reading her story. By the end of her book, the reader gains respect for how open and vulnerable she is and how that informs what they wish for themselves. And it is just this combination of vulnerability and insight that makes this book so rich and full of important information. Perhaps, more than anything else, Sam is a woman who is willing to be self-reflective; and the innovation that comes with self-reflection is an important lesson to be learned. It is through self-reflection that change can be made, lessons can be learned, and ultimately progress can take place in one's life.

This story is the real work of a woman who refused to acquiesce to fragility and stereotyping to become a warrior with a loud inner voice. One who resisted society's low expectations for her and demonstrated a vision of toughness, empowerment, faith, accountability, and a pursuit of excellence in her life and work.

Her book is an inspiration for all who wish to break through the challenges of life and become a vessel of hope and action.

Dr. Judith James, Ed. D, MA, LADC
Author of *"White Women Getting Real about Race"*

Introduction

We all have moments in life that make us feel powerless, and that's okay. It becomes a problem when we get stuck there. Have you ever felt powerless, broken, or lost? Have you ever felt like your back was against the wall and there was no way out? What about feeling stuck, or like life is kicking your ass? Have you ever considered taking your own life? Have you ever felt defeated or not good enough? Have you ever felt like you had no purpose? It's these kinds of feelings and beliefs that cripple us and kills our dreams. I am here to remind you that you have everything inside of you to live the life you deserve.

In my practice as a mental health therapist and addiction counselor, I have met thousands of women and most of them have one thing in common –pain. Many of them suffer from self-defeating thoughts and many of them have had experiences that make them feel powerless. I believe that we are born powerful, confident, strong, and resilient but it is our experiences that shape how we view ourselves. Unfortunately, some of us have negative belief systems and it takes away from who we could become. It's our own internal critic that keeps us feeling defeated.

Speaking about what it means to walk in power is a true passion of mine because I believe that we all deserve that. The topic of walking in power is important to me because when we create the best version of ourselves, we make the world a better place and we all know the world needs that right now. I don't know about you, but I'm exhausted by the chaos in today's world, and I must have coping skills and tools to make sure I am well. This book will provide encouragement and tools to help you get through life's toughest battles and come out on top every time. Some of us just need that push, or that word of encouragement, to keep us going and I hope this book provides that for you.

Introduction

If you're simply looking for a good read or hoping to learn something, I believe that this book can deliver that too. During my darkest moments, I needed a book, a sign, an encouraging word, anything to help me keep going so I understand the power of encouragement. I am not telling my story to receive sympathy; I want to be clear that this is a story about power – not pain. All the stories in this book are real events used for the purpose of inspiring another soul to be better. I put my real-life business out there to show people how not only did I allow things to have power over me, but also show how I built up the courage to take it back.

This book is a reminder that we all have a story, and in the end, we must own it. This book is a reminder that we all fall short sometimes, but we still deserve to win. This book is for the woman who is searching for ways to create a better life, but somewhere along the way lost her power. I just want you to know, girl you got this! I think it's important that we share our testimonies so those who are still struggling can see proof that they too can live in power and that they are not alone. You will read some stories that might be triggering, please take time and step away if you need to. Remember, you are in a safe place. God has allowed me to breakthrough and this book is my way of giving back.

I can tell you right now that stepping into your power will require you to always live in your truth. You're going to have to be willing to accept your reality for what is really is. Stepping into your power will require you to be confident and love yourself wholeheartedly. Stepping into your power will require you to make peace with your past and claim authority over your present.

Accepting who you used to be, and who you are, in this very moment is how you stay aligned with your truth. You must know who you are. Understanding what battles to fight is also essential when stepping into your power; it's the key to preserving your energy so you can be prepared for life's real battles. We must learn how to walk away and not engage in the things that were sent to destroy us. You must be confident in who you are so no one's opinion can shake you. A lot of people are out here searching for their power when all they need to do is step into it.

I hope after reading this book, you will always walk in power!

There are some dark moments in this book, but if you stay with me until the end, you will see that it is possible to come back from anything! I was in a very dark place, and I have been there many times, but I never allowed myself to stay there. If you are feeling down, right now, I urge you to get back up!

"You don't have to search for your power, but you do have to own it"
Sam Knight

Note From Author

Hey! I am happy you are here!

My name is Sumiko, professionally known as Sam. I am the author of this book. I use these names (Sumiko and Sam) interchangeably. I am a licensed addiction counselor and mental health therapist. I am the founder of a six-figure business, and the mother of three beautiful children. On the other side of that, I am a woman who struggles with mental health, I am amid pulling my business out of debt, and I struggled to write this book.

I wrote this book because it's something I have wanted to do for a long time. It was something that I knew needed to be done. I have a story of triumph and I know that someone needs to hear this so they can become empowered enough to create movement in their lives! As someone who was born into poverty and dysfunction, I know firsthand about life's ups and downs and how difficult it can be. I have worked with people from all backgrounds and pride myself on making connections. I strive to help people feel accepted and understood by providing a collaborative, non-judgmental, authentic experience.

I believe that you are the expert, and ruler, of your life; and that this book is a guide to help you process and find solutions to a better version of yourself. I wrote a book, sharing my personal moments of defeat, to give the blueprint of what it looks like to walk in power! I want to give the world my perspective on how one lives their life in power instead of pain. Yes, this book is all about encouragement and yes, I am rooting for you!

Areas of Interest/experience

Addiction, trauma, codependency, negative self-image, self-doubt, mental health issues, behavioral issues, domestic violence, incarceration, emotional issues, relational issues, generational trauma, the ideology of black people, and anger.

Education

Master of Arts Degree in Adlerian Counseling and psychotherapy with an emphasis on clinical mental health counseling

Bachelor of Science degree in addiction counseling at Metropolitan State University.

Okay so before we go on this journey, grab your blanket, grab some tea, and grab a seat because you're going to have to sit down for this one.

— 1 —

Childhood Sexual Abuse

My power began dwindling the moment I traveled my mother's birth canal and breathed in my first breath of air. I was born into brokenness. My mother was in the early stages of addiction and my father spent his days abusing women. They were no longer together by the time I was born, and my mom was living with my grandmother. I was the youngest of three children. On my mom's side, there was my brother Suki who was the oldest, my sister Suzie in the middle, and then there was me, Sumiko. We were figuratively steps because each child was two years apart from the next. Although we were born in Newburgh, New York, my mother decided to move us and raise us in St. Paul, Minnesota.

By the time we moved, my father was in prison serving a five-year sentence for a first-degree assault. He had shot a man and left him in a wheelchair. Remember the newfound addiction my mom had when she gave birth to me? Well, my father was also the man who introduced her to crack cocaine. These were the stories I was told about my father. And even though I knew he wasn't well enough to be an active part of my life, I still missed him and wanted to have him with me despite his faults. It was evident that my mom left Newburgh looking for something better, more than likely because she was tired of my father's shit. I think she was looking for a new start, as many of us do.

What could have been a great new start would never become one because my mother found herself, yet again, in the arms of an abusive man, only that this time, she didn't get away. When she met the man who would become my stepfather, he took her power away and she never got it back. There is no doubt in my mind that my mother suffered from codependency, she NEEDED a man and she needed him. His name was Omar, and he came into our lives to destroy us. He was light-skinned, with a nice smile, curly hair, and average in size. He was ten years younger than my mother and had one daughter whom he was not allowed to see. This should have been a red flag.

I remember meeting him and thinking to myself he was a nice guy. My mother met him at a nightclub and the rest was history. Within a few months, my mother moved him into our house. It was clearly not enough time to properly heal from the pain my father had caused her, and because of that, Omar took advantage of her vulnerability.

Once he moved into our home, he wasn't as nice as he'd been in the beginning. I remember the first time he whooped us. I was four, Suzie was six, and Suki was eight. He was babysitting us while my mom went to work. He had taken us to his mother's house to grab something; it was raining heavily and he told us to wait in the car.

"We should get out and play in the rain," I said, laughing. We all jumped out of the car and started dancing in the rain.

"It's raining, it's pouring, the old man is snoring," we sang, while dancing.

"Get the fuck back in the car!" Omar shouted, angrily. We all jumped back in the car.

"Didn't I tell you guys not to get out of the car? I'm beating you guys when we get back home."

I don't know how my siblings felt, but it was the first time, I felt scared. I had never been whooped before because my mom and grandparents did not whoop us. When we made it into the house, my sister Suzie tried to stop him.

"You can't whoop us, call my mom."

 "Oh, you want to talk back, just for that, you're the only one getting a whooping!"

He grabbed a metal spatula out of the drawer and started

You are Powerful

whooping Suzie on the back of her thighs until she begged him to stop. He walked out of the room, and we ran over to Suzie. She had the imprint of the spatula on her thigh. We told our mom as soon as she got home from work, but she didn't say much. We'd never been hit before and her response to my sister being hit by someone who was still practically a stranger was confusing. We soon realized the horror we'd experienced this rainy day, was a walk in the park compared to what was to come.

My mom quit working altogether after she got pregnant with Omar's first child. She decided she would rather stay home since the pregnancy caused so much sickness in the beginning. Even with her being home, it still didn't stop Omar from doing dirt. Not only was he not being supportive with his constant malicious rants and name-calling with us, but he even had my mom arguing with the family because he slept with my older cousin in the back of his van… RIGHT OUTSIDE OF OUR HOUSE! Believe it or not, my mom forgave him for that.

My mom gave birth to a baby girl and named her Monique. She was a beautiful baby; light-skinned, with no hair, and very mild-mannered.

One night, when she was still in her infant stage, Omar yelled out for me. I had no idea what he wanted, and when I realized he was in the bathroom, I really became confused. Still, I knew to be obedient, so I walked in. He was holding my baby sister and standing in front of the toilet exposed. He looked at me with a serious face and asked me to close the door. Then, he told me to hold his penis while he peed because "since he was holding the baby" he couldn't use his arms. At that moment, I honestly thought this was okay, and I never told my mom about it.

By the time I was seven years old, my mother had two children with Omar: Monique and Romae. My mother no longer talked about my father; she was building a new family. Omar called us names and made sure we knew that he was in charge. He treated his children better and made sure we knew that he did not love us the same. I still tried to like him and see him as a father, but his presence turned out to be one of my greatest challenges. He did things that took away my confidence and knocked down my self-esteem. He took most of my power. His molestation, his abuse, and his lack of empathy shattered me. His abuse only increased over time. One night, I was sitting up watching TV in the living room. We had a long sectional couch that could pretty much fit everyone on it. My mom was sleeping on one side with my baby sister Romae in her arms, and my other siblings were also on the couch asleep. The entire house was dark, other than the light from the TV. I looked up and there was Omar standing in the doorway of their bedroom; he waved his hand for me to come to him. I knew not to go in that room, but before I knew it, I was walking down the hall and entering their bedroom. After leaving that room, I had no power left. The next morning, I woke up and could hear my mother running bath water, she loved to take hot baths. I remembered last night and hurried to tell her what Omar had done to me.

I sat on the cold toilet seat staring at my mother as she soaked in the bathtub. Tears rolled down my face.

"Baby, what's wrong?" she said. "Tell mommy."

It took every ounce of my strength, but the words finally tumbled out. "Last night, Omar told me to come into the bedroom. When I did, he put his private part in my mouth."

To this day, the details are fuzzy, but here is what I do remember. I remember how afraid I was to go into that room. It was pitch black, and I could only see the edges of his body, like a frightening shadow. I remember him placing himself in my mouth and me standing as still as a statue until he went limp and removed himself. I remember him pushing my face away and ordering me out of the room.

The look on my mother's face reflected horror, but it also reflected something else; like disbelief, or like my words did not make sense. She sat up in the tub and stared at me. "He did what? Are you sure, Sumiko?"

You are Powerful

All I could do was nod. The tears streaked my cheeks, and I could taste salt in my mouth. "He did," I finally said.

She jumped out of the tub, water dripping off her body, and wrapped a towel around herself. She stopped at the bathroom door and said, "I don't know what to do. What do you want me to do?"

I shrugged my little shoulders and said, "I don't know." How could I know the answer to that? I was only seven years old. She hurried out of the bathroom without saying another word, and I heard her calling his name. "Omar!" I could hear anger and fear in that one word.

I stood up and went into the hall, unsure of everything around me. I was still crying. I didn't know what to do or where to go. All I knew was that you tell your parents when things like this happen. There was nothing to warn me of how difficult the aftermath would be. In my young mind, I would tell my mom, Omar would be arrested (or at least kicked out of the house), and we would move on. I heard shouting and then I heard my mother's voice and it caused me to take two unsure steps toward their bedroom.

My mother smacked her lips.

"That's your explanation? You were drunk!?"

"I was. I was drunk. I am sorry." It was Omar's voice, but he didn't sound sorry to me. "Don't worry. I'll apologize. Okay? I'll apologize." He said, with a smirk, as he headed to the door.

When I heard that and saw him heading my way, I turned around and walked into the living room. I sat on the edge of the couch and waited for what was next. Eventually, Mom came out of the bedroom and walked into the living room, her face red and the towel clinging to her body. She looked upset. "Go in. He wants to say something." She said, without looking at me.

I could not believe she was asking me to go back into that room. However, I did as I was told and walked into the bedroom. I stood in the doorway with my head down.

"Come by the bed." He was lying there, hungover and disgusting, smiling like someone who got caught with his hand in the cookie jar. I walked closer. He smirked, and said, "Hey, I am sorry about last night."

I remember looking into his eyes and him torturing me with his smile. I turned around and walked away. I walked out into the living room and sat on the couch. I sat there for hours afraid of what he could do next. That is what I can remember about the event that changed my life forever. I remember not really knowing what to feel or think. I did my best to move forward, but I was only seven years old.

What took my power - Being the victim of childhood sexual abuse

How I took it back - I found meaning in a situation that had none

I wish I could tell you that you don't have to find acceptance in something like this, but the truth is, if you don't, it's your peace that is disrupted. It's your life that will suffer the consequences of holding on to this. Yes, it's you who must pick up the pieces and that's the truth. This kind of pain can take all your power. There is no therapist, magic pill, or time that can heal you; you must do the work. You must find a way to accept, then forgive so you can whole-heartedly let this go. I allowed sexual abuse to impact most of my life and I had to forgive myself for that too.

I am an advocate for sexual abuse because I know it leaves permanent scars. Even at the age of thirty-six, I still have nightmares and flashbacks. Believe it or not, I still see him at times when I am being intimate with my partner, and I am still afraid of the dark. Trust for men is something I lack when it comes to being around my children. In the end, it left me with lifelong problems.

A lot of people would say that I am not healed, but the truth is, no matter how much healing a person does, the brain and the body do not allow us to forget trauma. I titled this chapter "Never the

Same" because sexual abuse changed the person I was forever. Sexual abuse happens so much that on some level, society no longer treats this as a big issue. It happens so much that child sex-trafficking is happening in our own communities. I have met men and women in their fifties and sixties still trying to heal from childhood sexual abuse. Many of them are hanging on to this trauma in ways they don't even understand. I personally lost all my power after being sexually abused for years.

I understand and I get it.

It was important that this topic be a part of this book because I know that sexual abuse takes away from our power. Sexual abuse can either make you better or break you completely. Let's be real, it's a painful experience and it almost broke me. Someone violated me, I can finally accept this part of me, and I have created meaning for this part of my life. If you are having a difficult time accepting the fact that you were sexually abused, you are not alone.

The truth I learned to accept is that there was nothing I could do to change the past, but I could heal and use this pain for power!

Tips on how to accept the things you cannot change:

Find acceptance : I found peace in accepting the fact that I could not change the past, but I could change the future. I had to stop looking for apologies and answers that I would never get. It sucked, but I had to accept the fact that my mother would never apologize and accept accountability the way I needed her to. She was not capable of loving me, and I had to accept that. I had to accept the fact that she allowed her boyfriend to sexually abuse me. I also had to accept the fact that she married him. It was either acceptance or self-destruction and I ultimately chose acceptance so I could move forward. Freedom is the gift of acceptance.

Forgive : If you are having difficulty accepting your sexual abuse, then more than likely, you're dealing with symptoms of resentment and hate. I personally used to get angry when people told me that I had to forgive. This statement helped me stay stuck. They would say things like, "You need to stop being angry" and I felt that I had the "right" to be angry. Let me be clear, you can still forgive someone and experience anger from time to time, that's okay. You just shouldn't obsess over it. Don't allow anyone to tell you how to forgive or what it looks like, do what works for you in a healthy way. Forgiveness is a self-designed process.

Find a way to heal : Healing means to return to a state of healthiness. I think it's safe to say that healing is also a self-designed process and its ongoing. There will be moments when you feel strong and then there will be moments when you feel triggered. I found my healing through helping others, receiving my own therapy and through spirituality. I also realized that if I did not heal, I would remain in an unhealthy state and I deserved to be a healthy person.

Let go and let God : Pain is something that people hold on to and it can become a person's identity. You can always tell when someone is holding onto pain because they project it into the world. They develop a victim mindset. I held on to mine for twenty years! If you're still holding onto pain, I want you to say this phrase right now out loud - **I release myself of pain and my past**. Say this to yourself every time your pain tries to come back.

"Healing after sexual abuse is like waking up after a car accident and learning that you may never walk again, only the scars are mental. I urge you to do the work so you can walk again" - **Sam Knight**

—2—

Generational Cycles

Aside from the sexual abuse in my childhood, I experienced a lot of things back then that caused me to struggle later in life. Seeing abuse and dysfunction was a norm for me growing up, so of course, it became a part of me. Once I realized how much my childhood was taking away from the woman I was trying to become, I was able to start changing it; but man, it was hard. My way of thinking was self-destructive, and it felt as though I was on a hamster wheel that I couldn't get off. All I could see when thinking about my future was defeat. I want to share a few more of my childhood stories to help you gain a better understanding of how I lost my power and why it took work to get it back.

So, you already know my mom did not leave Omar after I told her he violated me. He was still living with us, and his behavior only got worse. It had come to the light that he was not only sexually abusing me, but he was sexually abusing two of my mother's underage nieces which tore our family apart. My mother decided to hate her nieces because she felt the sex was consensual, so she never spoke to them again.

I will never forget the day I came home, and my older cousin was being kicked out of our house. As soon as I walked in the front door, all I could hear was my mom and my aunt Ruby banging on the bathroom door. Even back then, I still remember my aunt wearing nice wigs. She was dark-skinned, heavy set, always dressed to a tee, and covered in jewelry. In my eyes, she was my "rich" aunty. My mom was fair-skinned with short hair, thin with a small waist and a big butt; she was the black sheep of the family.

"Come out of there you slut!" My mom yelled.

She and my aunt were yelling at my sixteen-year-old cousin Draya who had got caught having sex with Omar. She had been sent to Minnesota to live with us due to a lot of girls wanting to fight her. She was mixed, high-yellow, nice body and she was sexually promiscuous. Even if she was willing, I was smart enough to understand that something was not right. She was still underage. I was shocked that my mom was yet again enabling this man's behavior. My negative thoughts about men started early on. Due to what I'd endured at the hands of a man, I thought all men were bad. In my eyes, they were all cheats, liars, and perverts. These negative beliefs about men impacted my behavior in future relationships.

Even though my mom and rich aunt seemed to be taking all their anger out on Draya, I was more upset with Omar. Really, why was this nasty grown-behind man having sex with his girlfriend's sixteen-year-old niece? If steam could visibly be seen from someone's head, I'm sure everyone in the house would have been shocked when they noticed me! Pissed wasn't even the word to describe how I felt. Omar walked through the house smiling despite all his terrible ways. I hated his smile, it traumatized me.

The next morning, I woke up to my brother and Omar fighting. He was punching my brother in the chest and calling him a "pussy". My brother and I were extremely close, so seeing him being punched and called a pussy, was again, traumatizing.

"Mom, can you get him off of him?" I pleaded with my mother to help my brother, but Omar was over 6ft tall and husky, so my mother was scared.

My brother cried and begged my mother to send him away. I guess my mother finally decided that my brother was better off living somewhere else. A few weeks later, my brother woke me out of my sleep.

"Hey, make sure you stay away from them boys and call me every day." His eyes were red from crying.

Quickly, I jumped up, grabbed him around his neck, and burst into tears. He squeezed me tight before leaving my bedroom and our home. He was moving to New York to live with his godmother. My mom did not want him and Omar getting into any more fights. I was hurt that my mother was sending my brother away instead of leaving Omar. It was never-ending. For years now, she'd over and over made a blatant decision to choose that man over her own flesh and blood. My anger was steadily growing towards her the more time passed. Not only had she sat back and allowed me to be molested, she'd allowed that man to physically assault my brother too.

I mean, really, where did she think he was when he was sneaking into my room?

One night, I woke up at about 3 a.m. to Omar trying to put his hands down my pants, I started kicking and to my surprise, he left. For the rest of the night, I lay there too terrified to go to sleep for fear that he was going to come back. When sleep started to overtake me, I did my best to curl into a fetal position against the wall so he could not get to me. So many nights, I lay there frozen as he fondled my breast or put his hands down my pants. Those nights, I screamed for my mother, but she never came. She was in the other room and in my mind, she was allowing this. Every time he came into my room, I learned that kicking and screaming were enough for him to leave me alone. I think it was the crack and alcohol that made him run off when I fought back. The paranoia that somebody would catch him was too much. He didn't want to be seen as a child molester.

I kept this disgusting secret between Omar, my mother, and me until I could no longer keep it. Although I did not have a bond with my older sister, she was the first person I told. I was shocked when she told me that Omar tried to touch her too. This may sound weird, but that was the first time I felt close to my sister. We hugged each other. She looked down at me and said, "I swear to never tell a soul, your secret is safe with me."

And I believed her.

We promised to take turns sleeping on the outside of the bed we shared to protect each other. She typically spent the night out, but she agreed to sleep with me going forward. Our bond was short-lived because I was getting older, and so was my sister. She found some local gang members that made her feel loved and accepted and she left our home for good. She only came home to shower and get clothes. I felt stuck. Everyone was leaving and I wanted to leave too, but they'd all left me to face Omar alone.

After school, I started spending most of my time with my best friend. She was my happiness because I could find none at home. Looking back, we both needed each other. I was tall and skinny, with short hair, and she was one of the biggest kids in the school. She was obese, short, and had short hair. We were an odd duo, but we loved it and did not care about anyone's opinion or anything really; and that made us well known, but not in a positive way. We were known as being "bad". We spent every day together for years. Her mom was always yelling, but from my perspective, she was a good mom. She worked, took care of the house, and she didn't use drugs. Her mom liked me, but you could tell she thought I was in trouble by the way she treated me. She couldn't understand why I was always out so late. She didn't know that I was trying to stay away from an abusive stepfather. I never told her either, I just allowed her to judge me. I didn't have the vocabulary then to explain what was going on at home. One of the last thoughts I can remember with Shay was me trying to sneak inside of her house.

"Ask my mom if you can spend the night," Shay said, she did not want me to go home.

"Hell no, you ask her, it's your momma," I whispered, loudly.

"Well, just hide in the closet, I saw that on a movie once. Let me tell Jay and Jamir so they do not get us caught." Shay had one older brother and one younger brother; we were both middle children. They both agreed to lie for her because she lied for them. As I sat in the closet, I could hear Shay's mom enter her bedroom.

"What the hell is going on up in here." Shay's mom yelled.

Shay busted out laughing, she was so damn silly. I did everything I could to hold in my laughter.

"What are you laughing about, who have you got in this closet?"

Mothers have a way of just knowing. She pulled me out of the closet and told me to walk my ass home.

"Listen, you two are always up to no good. There is school tomorrow, say goodbye and y'all walk her to the corner."

Instead of walking home, we all plotted on a new way for me to stay the night.

"Listen, I have another idea, we could tie sheets together and have you climb up the side of the house," Shay suggested.

" Girl, did you see that on TV, too?" "Yeah, I did," she laughed.

" Okay, we can try it." I agreed. I would try anything. As long as I did not have to be at home with Omar.

Once we made it back to their house, I crept to the side of the house and waited for the tied sheets to be thrown down from the window. I was always willing to try some crazy shit, why not, I had no fear. The sheets finally appeared, and I started climbing. As I looked up, I could see, Shay trying to hold in her laugh which eventually came out and she dropped me six feet. She had become so weak from laughing that she could no longer hold the sheets. I lay there in pain from the fall, and she hurried to the window still laughing.

"Are you okay?" She whispered.

"What the hell is going on?" Her mom yelled, running outside.

Once she realized what we had done, she allowed me to spend the night. That was life with my best friend, Shay. It was the connection with Shay that helped me believe that there was still hope for happiness. Later that night, my body was soaking wet as I jolted out of my sleep, sweating and scared. It was another nightmare. Oh yeah, I failed to mention, that was also a part of my childhood. I continued to have nightmares of Omar being on top of me, holding me down, and in these dreams, I couldn't get up or speak. These nightmares were intrusive and intense.

Shay was the one who woke me up.

"Girl, are you okay? You've been having nightmares all night".

"Yeah, I'm good, I'm not sure what I was dreaming about." Shay was my best friend, but she had no idea about Omar. Omar had put our family through things that I had only seen in the movies. However, this was my real life, a real-life nightmare. And what was even worse is that people thought he was a good guy. It was all a lie. My family was dysfunctional, and Omar was a monster! Not only was he evil and wreaking havoc on our lives, we were also dealing with generational trauma, sexual abuse, poverty, and mental health issues that I was not aware of as a child. I just knew I was not okay.

What took my power -Childhood trauma
Truth, I needed to accept- I was continuing the cycle

With all the chaos happening around me, I was like a deer in headlights. I was paralyzed on the inside. In my mind, I couldn't determine who I was, or why I was the way I was. I thought I was being strong by being able to endure all these traumas, but as I entered adulthood, I started to realize just how much my childhood had impacted my adult life. The same behaviors I told myself I would never engage in; I was now engaging in. The very things I vowed I would not allow as a woman, here I was dealing with it. Shame began to overtake me, and I became angry at myself for not being stronger.

Childhood trauma did exactly what it was supposed to do; it made me anxious, depressed, angry, and very reactive. I did not know how to recognize or have a healthy relationship. There were no boundaries in place for me because I had no idea how to create them. Hell, back then I didn't even know what a boundary was. Experiencing a lot of traumas at such an early age was like living in a nightmare. It felt like things would never get better, and I felt empty inside.

Generational cycles are the unhealthy patterns created and continued generation after generation. If you grew up in a dysfunctional family, like me, then you know how hard it is to break the "cycle". There is a saying, "the apple doesn't fall from the tree". This saying haunted me because as much as I told myself that I would be nothing like my mother, I became her more and more, unconsciously. My mother and father were unhealthy and so were my grandparents. My grandmother's mother did not know how to love her, my grandmother did not know how to love my mother, and my mother did not know how to love me. I knew in my heart that I would be the one to break these negative cycles. It is my responsibility to love my daughters and make them feel valued and important. It is my responsibility to be better and break negative family cycles or continue the cycles, but I do get to choose.

Tips on how to break the cycle

Change the repeated behavior: As much as I hated the things that I experienced as a child, I ended up doing a lot of the same things, it was natural. I acted out the same behavior I was raised in; yelling at my kids, allowing men to abuse me, being financially irresponsible and the list goes on. A hot mess wasn't even the word to describe who I'd become. My life had literally gone full circle and I was being the mom I once hated being around. I didn't even feel comfortable hugging my own child. If you really want to break the cycle, you must be mindful of your behavior so you can change it. You cannot use your childhood trauma as an excuse to repeat the same behavior. Even though I wanted to break the cycle of domestic abuse, I found myself in several abusive relationships. Repeating the same behavior came naturally to me and I had no idea how to disconnect myself from toxic behavior. My childhood experiences were enmeshed in who I was. I had to accept this. I had to admit to myself that I was a lot like my family, before I could change this behavior. It's still an everyday practice to live this new way of life, but it has been worth it.

Cut off toxic family members: To break through childhood trauma and generational cycles, you will have to be okay with people cutting you off and speaking bad about your name. I had to learn that not everyone wants change. We are taught to love family and accept them, no matter what. However, I do not agree. It's okay to call people out. It's okay to have constructive conversations. It's okay to stand up and say that you are choosing something different. It's okay to hold them accountable. Of course, you will have those family members that don't want better, those will be the ones telling you that you think you're better, simply because you want more. They will also be the ones making you seem like you're the one causing the destruction, yet they've been disrespecting you your entire life. It's okay to want better, stop feeling guilty for that.

Do the work: The truth is, I had a lot of healing to do. I did not trust men, I did not trust women, I did not trust family, and even worse, I didn't trust myself. In my mind, I questioned everything and everybody. Every reaction I had was based on my trauma instead of the situation at hand. This made me angry at the world and I destroyed relationships because of it. I destroyed everything around me. There were things within me that I needed to change, or the cycle would continue, and I could no longer blame the generation before me.

— 3 —

The Power of Addiction

Aside from all of Omar's drama, he and my mother were addicted to drugs. They never had extra money because it all went to drugs. I never got to buy books out of the bookstore, and I never had money for field trips. There were many times I remember wishing I had been given five bucks to buy myself some snacks, or a book from the bookstore. It was these experiences and so many more that made me feel inferior. My mother was on welfare with a crack addiction and seven children, there was nothing to look forward to in my mind.

Omar worked, but most of his money supported their drug habit. They didn't care about having money for laundry and we never did things outside of the home. One day, I remember vividly washing my clothes out in the sink and placing them on the heater to dry. Back then, I can honestly admit I hated myself. I had already been through a lot, but my adversity was just beginning.

I will never forget the day my mom busted into our room and yelled, "Get down on the floor!"

She quickly turned off all the lights and then gunshots rang out. Someone was shooting up our house because Omar had allegedly raped some young woman. My mom told us all the next day that we were moving back to New York in a few days. At the time, I wasn't sure why we had to move so suddenly, I just knew that whatever Omar did, it was serious enough that we had to leave our home.

A few days before we left Minnesota, it was one of my friends who opened my eyes to my mother's addiction to crack cocaine, she confirmed my thoughts. It was my neighbor, Nay-Nay. She was younger than me, but she knew more than any ten-year-old should know. I learned a lot of grown-up things from her, but this day, she confirmed something that I had been curious about.

"It's getting late, we should head back home now," I warned.

Nay-Nay laughed, "Girl, our moms are smoking crack, they are not thinking about us, we can stay out longer."

"My mom does not smoke crack!" I was offended she would even say something like that about my mom, even though deep down I wondered if it was true.

"If you don't believe me, the next time your mom goes into the bathroom and comes out looking all wired, that's how you will know. That look means she's high."

On the walk home, I did very little talking. My mind was running a mile a minute and I just wanted to know the truth once and for all. I will never forget what I witnessed that night. It's something you just don't forget, and it was another layer of my dysfunctional childhood. I can't tell you how I knew about crack, but I can tell you that I knew.

While sitting on the couch that night, I noticed my mom making several trips to the bathroom. My curiosity got the best of me, and I wanted to know if my mom was smoking crack. As quietly as I could, I tip-toed to the bathroom and looked through the keyhole. She was sitting on the toilet with what appeared to be a piece of a TV antenna, and she put it in her mouth. There was a pipe in one of her hands and a lighter in the other. She lit it up and began smoking it like a cigarette. I fell to the floor with my back against the wall and decided, at that moment that I was going to confront her. She came out of the bathroom, and I jumped up scaring her.

"What were you smoking in there?" I inquired.

She smacked me in the face and screamed, "Don't you ever disrespect me; I am still your mother."

Holding my face in complete shock, I ran away and cried myself to sleep. I hated my life. My mother no longer worked, which was also a side effect of her getting high. She was a stay-at-home mom with seven kids. Omar worked and used that to control her. He always called her lazy, and a bitch, and most times the words were used together in whatever hateful sentence he spewed at her for the day. He broke her down with his words and then got her high to numb the pain he'd caused. It was their cycle, and in her eyes, it was love. At the time, I did not realize that addiction was a progressive disease and that my mother's illness would only get worse as time went on. It was traumatizing to see her lose weight, lose her hair, and walk around the house high. To this day, I can still picture the look in her glassy eyes, and I can still recognize the smell of crack. Trust me, the smell is atrocious.

Eventually, she became so wrapped up in her addiction, and Omar, that she neglected our basic needs. We went days without bathing, days with our hair uncombed; most of my hair had fallen out and I was teased for that. The names they called me made me feel so small. Bald head was a name I heard often, which was yet another thing that took away from my confidence. She struggled to keep up with the laundry and the cleanliness of the house. She was also never at school events. Her addiction took my power away because it made me feel worthless. In my mind, I would never be enough for her, and I often wondered why. I hated her for staying with Omar and for smoking crack. For obvious reasons, I just could not accept the fact that my mother was a crackhead. The older I got, the more her addiction grew, as well as the sickening love she had for the monster she couldn't let go of. I was the last of my father's kids, and the one person standing in the way of her happiness with Omar.

On top of learning about my mother's addiction, I would have to say good-bye to my friends. I will always remember how I had to break the news to them.

"Alright class, it's time, let's sing our hearts out," our teacher said.

We all stood up and sang R, Kelly's song, "I believe I can fly". Those types of moments helped me feel a sense of normalcy and I had some hope. Everyone in the class was handed an award that day. I won the funniest classmate because I was always playing and running my mouth cracking jokes. I was also known for being a bad kid because of it, too.

After all the excitement died down, I made my heartbreaking announcement, "Okay guys, I have to tell you all that my mom has decided to move our family back to New York."

Shay burst into tears, "You can't leave me, I can't live without you!" We all hugged and stood outside taking pictures, I was sad because

I knew that this meant good-bye forever and I hated saying good-bye to people I felt connected to. Even though I was young, I understood that this would be our last moments. Although we all said we were going to keep in contact, I knew with us all still being kids, that was highly unlikely. I was trying to keep it together, but leaving Shay also changed me because I still hate good-byes today.

I appreciate seeing them on Facebook now! For the most part, I coped with life through my friends. I needed them more than they could have ever known. Later, I found out that Omar and his best friend did, in fact, rape a girl in our community and he was scared that she might figure out who he was and call the police.

The next morning, we woke up at the crack of dawn to get on the Greyhound bus and that was the end of Minnesota for a while. After a long bus ride from Minnesota, we finally arrived at my grandmother's house in New Windsor. I was excited because New York was so different. It was the end of my life with Omar, or so I thought, but not with dysfunction. I had high hopes that we would soon move back to Newburgh. I loved Newburgh and was honored to have been born there. It's a small place in the middle of New York.

I hated living in New Windsor, and I wanted badly to move back to Newburgh. Newburgh was jumping. The people, the food, the air, everything was way more exciting there. The girls were confident and had big hair and big earrings. I had on baggy clothes, stud earrings, and a short ponytail. The great news was that I could at least still attend school in Newburgh. As a matter of fact, I had to, because

New Windsor was so small.

I stood in the gym so quietly that everyone started to notice. "Hey, your Malcolm's sister from Minnesota, right?"

"Come hang with us." One of the older girls in the gym class allowed me to follow her and her crew around.

My family was popular, so people hung out with me just off their popularity. I didn't mind, I was happy to be a part of the crew.

I had four brothers in total, three from my dad and one from my mother, but I loved them all the same. My oldest brother on my dad's side, Pay, was the most popular. He was your typical, drug dealer, boss, playa, and real street dude. He had his pick of women, cars, clothes, shoes, and money. He did not go to school, he stood on William Street. He was the "MAN". Then there was Suki, he was my mother's son (the one she sent away) and at one point my best friend, but the older we got, the more distant we became. He was a pretty boy, and my two younger brothers were Mike and Tony. They were all light-skinned, slim build, tall, and handsome. Of course, looking back, it hurts to know how bad everyone had failed them, but what was worst was watching them fail themselves. They were truly good people but did what they thought they needed to do to survive.

When you grow up in poverty, you don't live for tomorrow, you live for the day. In your mind, there is no hope, and there is no possibility. Having parents who are addicted to crack and no one speaking life into you makes it difficult for any child to grow up and be productive in this world. My brother Tony suffered the most out of all of us. He was in and out of the boy's home because he did not attend school. He would run away from these homes, and we would always hang out when he was on the run. We had all been abandoned by our parents.

It was crazy, but I had contact with my siblings by running into them mostly in the streets. We were all sleeping on someone's couch, except for Pay. My brothers selling crack cocaine caused them to ultimately spend over a decade in federal prison.

I understood why they sold drugs and a part of me still does. It was a way to provide money so they could have food in their bellies and clothes on their back. Young black men are condemned for selling drugs and joining gangs, but I understood and even today can understand why people give in to this kind of behavior. Being around drug dealers was a part of my neighborhood, it was normal. Of course, I know now that there is nothing "normal" about selling drugs. I understand now that drug dealing is the easy way out.

When I lived in Minnesota, I saw things, but they were nothing compared to the things I saw in Newburgh. It was filled with poverty, drug dealers, crackheads, abandoned buildings, and abandoned kids.

Since I was back in Newburgh, I was finally able to meet my father. I met him when I was twelve years old, and it was awkward. I was excited and hopeful to have one parent, but he was also incapable. He smoked crack and he had severe mental health issues. I met him but a relationship never developed. He didn't drive or have a car, so my uncle Jimmy picked me up from my grandmother's house to meet him for the first time.

"Come on, Uncle Jimmy is outside with grandma Nookie," my mom was yelling for me to go outside.

They were picking me up to meet my father for the first time. Up until now, I only imagined who he was, how he looked, walked, and talked. On the way from New Windsor to Newburgh, I rested my head on the window as Mary J. Blige's song, "You are everything" was playing on the radio. We pulled up to Benkard and there he was standing out front, I knew it was him. I got out of the car and his smile was big as the sun. He was tall and light-skinned, and he had fine hair.

"Hey baby girl, well, I'm your father and it's nice to meet you!" he said in a joking manner. I knew at that moment that I had got my humor from him.

There I was, meeting my father for the first time at twelve-years-old. We joked around and laughed with my grandmother and uncles. It made sense why I was so silly, my father joked the entire time.

I was shy and nervous. My grandmother, great-grandmother, and uncles all sat around and gave their opinions on who I looked like and who I reminded them of.

"You shake your leg just like your father," my grandmother observed.

Shaking my leg had become a coping skill for me, I think it helped me stay calm in anxious situations. Living in New York, I saw my father and his family more and more, but somehow, we never maintained a relationship. I guess too much time had passed. It hurt not to be loved by them, I was hoping that I would find love there. The truth is that my father and his entire side of the family had abandoned me and it made me feel unloved.

I did, however, build a strong bond with my half-siblings. I wanted to go to Newburgh every weekend because I had fun there. My mother's mom lived in New Windsor which is a suburb compared to Newburgh. My grandmother hated Newburgh. She was a bitter old lady. She did not want me going to chill with my family in Newburgh, she thought that Newburgh was to blame for my mother's shortcomings.

"You don't have no business being in Newburgh, that's where your mother was hanging and look how she turned out."

My grandmother was always putting my mother down because of her addiction to drugs and how she allowed men to treat her. In my eyes, she was the reason for my mother's pain and shortcomings. She abused my mother as a child, and she allowed a family member to sexually abuse my mother. I wanted to stay in Newburgh and not go back to New Windsor. I wanted something different, and I did not care that my grandmother hated Newburgh.

"Mom, can I please go to Newburgh?"

"Your sister is literally trying to get on a greyhound bus back to

Minnesota, can you please leave me alone right now?"

Samara screamed, "I hate it here, I do not want to live with you, or Omar because I know you're going to allow him to come back soon like you always do. I hate you!"

My sister cried until my mother finally gave in and decided that she could go back to Minnesota. She had talked to one of my sister's adult friends who had promised to take care of her. I watched as my older sister got in a taxi and rode away headed to the bus station. She was only fourteen years old; I didn't see her again for years. I was sad that my mother was abandoning her, but at this point, I kept on going as if the chaos didn't exist. I learned how to live in that space, it was the only way to survive. I mastered not giving a fuck.

We all moved on like she never existed. My mom finally found a place in Newburgh, and I was happy as hell to be getting away from my grandmother. The sad part was that Omar was on his way from Minnesota to live with us. Once we moved to Newburgh, I changed. I started hanging out with friends more and I was never home.

What took my Power - Having a mother who was addicted to drugs

Truth, I needed to accept - She would never be the mother I expected her to be

I want to start this off with a fact about what the world has to say about a child growing up with an addicted parent.

Fact-(*https://thearbor.com/blog/how-addiction-affects-children/*) A recent Harvard University research study determined that children whose parents use drugs and misuse alcohol are three times more likely to be physically, sexually, or emotionally abused and four times more likely to be neglected than their peers. Parents who suffer from addiction often struggle to set priorities and fail to meet even the basic needs of their children.

As you can already see from the previous chapters, all these things were true for me, and they made me feel powerless. I hated going to school with my hair undone and I hated wearing clothes out of the dirty clothes basket. Aside from my basic needs not being met, my emotional, physical, and mental health needs were also neglected. My mother never hugged me, and she rarely told me that she loved me.

She brought me around drug dealers and thankfully, none of them raped me or asked her to exchange me for drugs. As you will read in a later chapter, one of her female drug dealers took me in and allowed me to live with her. There was also a lot of shame, and I was honestly embarrassed by my mother for a long time. It hurt to see her addiction have power over her and I think that is what made me feel powerless. It was because what she was dealing with was something I could not change or control.

Tips on how to cope with having a parent who is addicted to drugs or alcohol:

Acceptance: I have found a way to accept it, but it took my power for a long time. If you love someone who is addicted to drugs, or alcohol, I know how exhausting and scary this is. You feel helpless when you cannot help the person you love. I have met thousands of addicts throughout my career, and I have seen how hard they fight for sobriety, trust me addiction is powerful. The power of addiction has proven to be the most powerful trap known to mankind. I used to hate my mother for not "just quitting". I understand now that it's not that simple and I have accepted this part of me.

Try to gain an understanding: Working in drug rehabilitation centers changed my perspective and it did help me accept my mother's addiction. I now understand the power of addiction and that even when a person truly wants to quit, the craving is stronger. You also must understand that drugs make people feel good. My mother had been through a lot of her own trauma and unfortunately, just like many, she found healing in crack cocaine. She loved it; it took away her pain, worries, and accountability. I had to accept her addiction and stop hating her for it. If you have a loved one who is struggling with addiction, try to accept, get support, set boundaries, and love yourself first. Learn how to accept them for who they are.

Accept them for who they are : When I was younger, I wanted my mother to be the mother I expected her to be. I wanted her to be strong and work on her sobriety. It angered me to no end that she wasn't who I needed her to be. I finally got to the point of accepting her for who she is and realizing that I could not change her.

— 4 —

Abandonment

If you've ever been abandoned by someone you loved and trusted, then you know how much power being abandoned can take from a person. Abandonment can take your power because it makes you feel insecure and unworthy. It causes you to have trust issues and doubt yourself. All these issues were true for me. Trust for anyone was a no go for me and I was paranoid. I never believed that anyone truly cared about me and although I struggled in relationships, I struggled to be alone, too. Eventually, I would use men for comfort just like my mom.

Dream was my first relationship and my first experience with love and heartache. Prior to him, I never liked a boy before, but he was so fine! He was dark-skinned with good hair, and perfect features. His hair was shiny and long, all the girls wanted him and his older brother. In the beginning, I was so scared to talk to him because I still wore baggy clothes and lacked confidence. The girls at my school were prettier than me. We had 8th period together, which was math class, and that became my favorite part of the day. I sat down for class and my first crush walked in ten minutes late, flirting with the teacher. He sat behind me, and I could feel the butterflies start a raging war in my stomach.

There was a tap on my shoulders, and he whispered, "Yo, aren't you Pay and nem sister?"

I nodded; it was the only response my nerves would allow. "Yo, you got some more gum, and why you so quiet?"

I let out a nervous giggle, "I don't have any more gum and I'm shy."

That day, I walked out of that class in complete awe. There was not a day that passed by that I didn't think about him, but he had a girlfriend, and she was prettier than me. She also had long hair and she dressed nicely.

Then one day, this happened...

"Girl, did you hear that Dream and his girl broke up? You have to ask him out before it's too late," my girl Sienna said.

When I tell you I took that information and ran with it, I did! Dream hung out on Liberty Street, and I knew that if I waited by the corner store, I would run into him. While sitting on a stoop, talking to my friends, he came flying down the street on a bike. Even though I was star-struck, I asked him, "Do you want to be my boyfriend?"

"Yeah," he laughed, "I never had a girl ask me out."

To this day, I wholeheartedly believe he only started dating me to make his ex-girlfriend mad, because she left him for another guy, but I didn't care, I just wanted him; I wanted to be loved. Looking back, that was the start of my developing codependency, but back then, I couldn't see it coming, I didn't have the knowledge. I thought I was a young girl experiencing her first crush, but I was too sick for anything to be normal.

Daily, I started chilling with Dream. He was always at his older sister Margie's house; she was young and allowed us to kick it there. Dream was my peace away from home. I needed him. I even convinced my mom to move to his side of town so I could see him more. She had been approved for section 8 and my friend's old house was for rent right on Dreams block. Once we moved in, I was right there with Dream. His older homeboys hung out on the end of the corner in Newburgh and we called it the "the block".

All the older cats were nice to me, they thought that Dream was a young player in the making and in the hood, that was encouraged.

I felt so close to him to the point I stopped hanging out with my friends. I also told him my secret.

"Man, I hate that nigga," I hissed, eye balling Omar as he came into the neighborhood slowly.

"Who, your step-pops?"

"Yeah, but he is not my step-pops, he sexually abused me," I relented.

Dream jumped up like he had just heard something unbelievable. "What the fuck you mean? Do your moms know?"

"Yeah, but she loves that nigga's dirty drawers, and she isn't leaving him."

"Nah man fuck that, and you got to live with this nigga? Yo, go to the house, I'll be back".

"Wait, what are you about to do?" I called out to him, but it was too late.

He ran off to his homeboys and I walked to my porch. Omar pulled up, banging his music loud like a real cocky dude. I noticed that Dream and his homeboys were walking down the street and they did not look happy. They walked up on Omar's car, pulled him out, and started beating the shit out of him. I looked back and I could see my little sisters crying. I jumped up and begged them to stop, which they did.

"Nigga you a bitch and you're not allowed to walk through the block anymore" One of Dream's homeboys made it clear that sexual predators are not welcome on their block.

I just stood there.

Omar had knots all over his head and was bleeding from the face. I ran up to the block to see Dream, embarrassed at the same time because his friends knew my "secret". They didn't say anything to me, they were listening to their beatbox, smoking, drinking, and laughing about what they had just done. Dream came off the stairs.

"You good, yo?" He had the sweetest eyes. "Yeah," I gushed.

He hugged me, and for the first time said, "I love you." "I love you, too."

Every experience like this made me fall harder. Looking back this kind of unhealthy attachment to a boy was the onset of my codependency. I started depending on a man to make me happy.

The next day, I woke up to Omar screaming from the pain and injuries that he got while getting beaten up. My mother was right there taking care of him, and it hurt to watch her love him so much. She called me into their room, and I walked in with my hands folded across my chest.

"Sumiko, come here for a second, your aunt Bay called saying she is sick, and she wants you to help her around the house for the summer."

"So, when do I leave?" I asked, not really wanting to be in her room long.

"You're going to have to leave on the last day of school."

As much as I loved Newburgh, I was excited to visit Minnesota because I left my family behind. After school ended on the last day of school, Omar drove me to the Greyhound bus station because my mother never learned how to drive. As I sat on the Greyhound bus listening to my Walkman, I thought about being back in Minnesota and got excited again; I kind of missed it. The bus ride from Newburgh to Minnesota was two days because of the stops. My cousin ReRe picked me up from the Greyhound bus station, and as soon as I got in the car, I could tell something was wrong. She pulled over to a parking space and my heart started beating faster and faster. I know now that I was having a panic attack.

"Miko, I know Omar has been sexually abusing you and your sister," she blurted.

My heart dropped and I could not make eye contact with her. As tears rolled down my face, I leaned my head onto the car window.

After a few minutes of silence, she started the car and pulled off. I rode to our destination in silence. As soon as I walked into my aunt's house, I saw my sister, my brother, and my aunt sitting around her dining room table. I was shocked to see my brother Suki because he lived in Newburgh!

My aunt Bay broke the silence. "Sit down, we need to talk." She watched me as I grabbed a chair and took a seat. "We know Omar has been touching you and Samara."

Like a kettle about to sound the alarm that it was at a boil, anger started to build up, because my own sister shared something that was for me to share. That was my choice. I folded my arms and just sat there with tears rolling down my face. Looking back, I think it was more hurt and shame than anger.

"I don't know what you're talking about, that's a lie."

"Girl, we already know he tried to make you suck his private, your mom is sick and you're not going back home."

As tears rolled down my brother's face, he asked, "Why didn't you tell me?" as he rammed his hand on the large dining table.

I could no longer contain my anger, "Fuck all of you, this shit is not true."

"We know it's true and how dare you curse at me!" Aunt Bay yelled.

My aunt was a Jehovah's witness and cursing was not allowed in her house, especially from a child. They all walked me to the basement and let me have my space. I asked for a phone, called my mom, and before I knew it, I was back on the Greyhound bus. My mom had Omar's sister purchase me a one-way bus ticket back home. To escape without causing alarm, I convinced my aunt and siblings that I was okay and just wanted to go spend the night with a friend. Once I got to my friends, I had Omar's sister pick me up later that evening. There I was, back on the Greyhound bus. I just laid my head on the glass window and wondered what was going to happen after all of this occurred. Would my mom finally leave Omar? Would things be better or worse?

Omar picked me up from the bus station and I just sat there silent, we both did. When we got home. I ran straight to my room, as I lay there looking at the ceiling, my door opened.

"I just want to say thank you," Omar said, thanking me for keeping what he'd been doing to me a secret.

I shot up, and yelled, "I didn't lie for you! I lied for my sisters and my mother, now get the fuck out of my room."

Every time I had to take a loss for my mother, I became angrier. I thought that she would leave him and finally see that the "secret" was out. She did the exact opposite and held on to him even more. She forbade me to talk to my aunts or older cousin; the only people who loved me. At the time, I thought that they were trying to hurt my mother and take custody of her kids, but my mom was sick, and they were trying to help me. My mother had convinced me that "she" was the victim.

The summer had passed, and before I knew it, it was a new school year. It was 8th period, and the day was almost over. I was laughing and goofing around in class. The classroom phone rang, and it was the office calling for me.

"Sumiko, the principal's office called, they want to see you."

As I walked to the office, I joked and played around with other students. I honestly thought nothing of this office visit because I was always in trouble. As I walked into the principal's office, I saw two white guys that looked like the police, and my mood went from happy to pissed off real fast! I instantly realized that this was not a regular visit to the principal's office.

"Sumiko, we're here because we got a call from someone who claims that you're being sexually abused."

I remember feeling sick to my stomach and scared of what was to come next. As I screamed on the inside, before I knew it, I was already uttering words that I would resent later in life.

"No that's a lie, I am not being sexually abused."

I couldn't bring my mouth to speak that truth because it was something that I wanted to forget. I was in DENIAL. I hated not telling the truth but all I could think about was my mother, my sisters, and what their life would be like if I told these white men about what was really going on at home. I wanted them to have a better childhood than I had and so I kept this secret and lived with it internally. I had no idea that one day, I would resent my little sisters for this because we turned out to be divided in the end. They had a father who supported them; and well, me, all I had was "me". As soon as they allowed me to leave the office, I burst into tears because I still did not know what would be next. I busted through the front doors of the school and ran home with my heart racing a million miles per hour. I was scared and it felt like the secret I had been hiding for so long had been exposed for the world to see. I did not want to face this and in my opinion, no child should have to face this kind of shit. My mom wasn't home when I got there, so I went and lay down on my bed. I closed my eyes for a moment and when I opened them, Omar was standing there naked.

"Thank you," he smirked.

I jumped up so fast and yelled, "Fool, get the fuck out of my room! I denied it for my sisters and mother, not you!"

He walked away and I resumed my previous position on the bed and into a deep thought. This fool was really thanking me for not telling the world about what he did. I could feel the anger boiling over like water that had been left on a stove too long. It's no wonder I have a hard time just walking away from people and things that have me fucked up. However, I had no tolerance for stress at this point, and I was reactive as hell.

Later that evening, my mom came home in a panic, "Miko, what happened at school today?

"I don't know, two white dudes said they got a report that I was being sexually abused."

"That bitch Bay called them people on me," she hissed.

And I have no idea why, but I was completely flabbergasted by her response.

Bay was my mom's oldest sister and the two of them hated each other. The next morning, I woke up and my mom told me I could stay home from school. We sat on the couches and that's when she said the words that replayed in my mind for years.

"Yeah, I talked to the two cops who spoke to you, and we have to leave Newburgh because they said they are investigating the claim. They said Omar could no longer live in this home until they figure this out."

"Okay, so he should get his own place then!" I said with complete disgust and disbelief, "Fuck you, and I am not leaving Newburgh".

"Okay, well you can go live in New Windsor with your grandmother," she replied, nonchalantly. "Miko, I am marrying Omar this Friday."

Trust me, I knew what pain felt like, but hearing her say those words that day crushed my spirit. My body went numb, I could not believe the words she'd spoken. It felt like life was one big ball of hurt and disappointment. What she did to me felt worse than a mother who simply did nothing, it was something that impacted every piece of me beyond my control. I looked at her and of course, I did not show hurt, I showed anger. My eyes filled with tears, I looked her straight in the eyes and asked, "How could you marry him after what he did to me? If you marry him, I will never forgive you and I am definitely not coming to that wedding."

"Well, Sumiko, I have said sorry a million times, I don't know what else to do, but I am marrying him."

At this point, the tears were lapping under my chin. I quickly wiped my face and ran upstairs. I don't know where the idea came from, but that was the first time I attempted to take my own life. Opening the medicine cabinet, I grabbed a bottle of cough syrup and guzzled the entire bottle. Initially, I didn't feel anything, but moments later, the room started to spin. I could no longer talk, and everything was moving in slow motion. Finally, I made it to my bed and fell asleep. Surprisingly, I woke up the next morning, and in one last effort to try to make my mom choose me, I told her that I tried to kill myself.

She just looked at me and said, "You better stop playing with your life!"

There was no suggestion for therapy, no hug, and certainly no I love you. She just could not be the mother I needed her to be. Even though I told her that she could leave, deep down inside, I was really saying "I need you, please don't leave." I was too young back then, however, and I didn't have the communication skills to express my true feelings.

The day they left, I remember kissing my little sisters goodbye and watching them all get in the taxi to head to the bus station. My heart was broken, and I hated my life. I watched them pull off together, and I turned around and looked at that big empty house. Then, I walked back inside and sat in the living room in the recliner chair listening to Lauryn Hill's CD, The Miseducation, and I can remember the phrase in that song that made me have a spiritual moment with God! I think it was at that moment that God sat with me, and I was able to fall asleep.

> "Now I may have faith to make mountains fall. But if I lack love, then I am nothin' at all
>
> I can give away everything I possess.
>
> But left without love, then I have no happiness I know I'm imperfect
>
> And not without sin
>
> But now that I'm older all childish things end and tell him

> Tell him I need him
>
> Tell him I love him
> And it'll be alright
> Tell him…

That moment hurt like hell. I remembered my aunt telling me that God had the power to make anything better, and I believed that it was the only hope I had left. Music and God were two things I could always depend on. It was something spiritual about someone else singing and understanding my pain. The lyrics to that song reminded me that I was nothing without love. I bawled up and cried until I fell asleep in that chair. Hours later, I woke up and looked around that fully furnished empty four-bedroom house and thought, who leaves behind a thirteen-year-old in a whole house? It was the Lauryn Hill's CD, The Miseducation, that got me through that moment. Her music made me feel like there was hope.

What took my power - Abandonment by the people who were supposed to love me

Truth, I needed to accept - My family did not love me
"It's hard to carry on when no one loves you"- 2pac

The above line is one that I felt often as a child and as an adult. Not having love from my parents, or community, made it so hard to keep going. I didn't feel valuable, lovable, or important. My mother leaving me was my first real experience with abandonment (my father and his family were never there, so with them I felt rejected). It hurts to my core to be abandoned by her, but it was something I could not control. To make matters worse, everyone in my family and the community had abandoned me. I can admit that this made me feel unworthy, angry, and bitter. It made me not trust people, I always thought they would leave. It made me clingy and guarded in relationships.

Having abandonment issues also impacted my parenting. It was hard for me to hug my daughter as she got older. I had to teach myself how to love because it was easy to turn my vulnerability off. Healing this part of me was necessary in order to take my power back and love myself more.

Tips on coping with abandonment issues:

Realize that you can live without them: When someone abandons you, you feel like you can't go on or be whole without them.

Realize that you matter: I had to realize that I was enough no matter who walked out of my life. Realizing that I was okay no matter what made me stronger, made me feel peace and eventually made me better. My mother walking out on me took my power. I felt alone. The first step to taking your power back, after abandonment, is realizing that you are never alone. I would also challenge you to accept the reality of the situation. Give yourself positive affirmations and build yourself a team for support.

Practice Self-love: It took me almost two decades to realize that no one could love me like I could love myself. I was searching for something that was within. When you love yourself, you have a clear understanding of what you deserve.

Practice Affirmations: When you're abandoned by someone, it makes you feel insecure and not good enough. I was introduced to affirmations a few years ago and they have helped me speak life into myself. When my family abandoned me, I felt unlovable. I started to write and tell myself that I am lovable, and it has helped so much. Do this daily and it will change your life.

Get into therapy: Having abandonment issues will require you to do some internal work. It will require you to process things and find a better understanding of your shortcomings in relationships and within yourself.

— 5 —

The Mindset of Hopelessness

After my mom and siblings left, there were only a few days of me living in that big house alone before someone called child protection services. While sitting in the living room looking out of the window, a white man wearing a suit approached the front door. Instead of answering, I rushed out of the back door straight to Dream's house and never looked back. Dream's mom, who obviously didn't like me, advised me to go to my grandmother's house in New Windsor like my mom had asked me to do. His mom was so mean to me. She more than likely didn't like me because she felt I was too young to take my relationship with her son so seriously.

She stood in the middle of the screen door with her arms folded across her chest and stated full of attitude, "Sumiko, you know you can't stay here, I am not trying to be a grandmother."

"I know." I retorted, and with that, I turned and walked away.

After walking around aimlessly for a few blocks, I finally called my grandmother. She sent my uncle, Gary, to pick me up. Living with my grandmother was the last thing I wanted to do because she talked bad about my mother, and she was strict. She would never allow me to visit Newburgh and my happiness was there. Nevertheless, it was either do that or become homeless and risk being put into the system, so I sucked it up and made do.

"Hey Muppet," My grandmother greeted as soon as I walked into the house. Muppet was the nickname she gave me as a baby.

My grandmother had red skin with long fine hair, and she was short and heavy set. She hated my mother for having so many kids and for being on welfare and drugs. She made it known to whoever would listen that she was ashamed of her. She had zero boundaries with her words, and with them, she would cut you as if she was carrying the sharpest machete. Unfortunately, she never realized that talking about my mother did not help me.

"Your momma doesn't want to do anything, but smoke crack and allow that nigga to control her life," she hissed, not too long after I got there.

Despite everything my mother had put me through, I was beyond confused emotionally. I hated her but loved her at the same time. Learning how to detach from her seemed impossible.

"Fuck you, you can't talk about my mother like I am not even here," I yelled. And with that, I got up and ran out the front door, and I did not see Big Mom again until I was pregnant with my first child which was about three years later.

That day, I walked and ran all the way to Newburgh, which was several miles away. I had a lot of time to think during that journey. The tears seemed endless, and I concluded (once again) that I didn't want to live anymore. Going back to New Windsor was simply not an option for me, no matter how scared I was to be out on the streets. Eventually, I decided to go to my mother's old drug dealer's house who just so happened to be a woman who really liked me. I knocked on her door.

Trudy answered, "Hey, Miko, what's going on?"

Tears escaped me before I even realized it, "I don't have anywhere to go."

"Come on in here, you can share a room with Brit Brat," she said without a moment of hesitation.

Her name was Trudy, she was about 350 pounds and only had one leg after having to get her leg cut off due to catching an infection that she could not go to the hospital for due to a warrant for her arrest.

She was so nice to me, and so was her daughter. When I walked into the home, Trudy showed me to the room where I would be sleeping, and I sat on her bed staring into space. Brit Brat came and stood right in front of me, "I always wanted a big sister, come on let me show you around our room."

Trudy bought me school clothes, took me to family events, and always gave me money for my pocket. The only problem with living with her was that her family hated the fact that she treated me like I was her own. I constantly found myself having to fight her family because of jealously. After living with Trudy for several months, my time had run out. It happened when I was physically attacked by her niece who was jealous, and I decided that I could no longer live in that environment.

"Trudy, your niece just literally called me a bitch and homeless, I do not want to keep dealing with this."

"Hold on a sec, let me call her around the corner so we can talk about what's going on."

Moments later, Barnes walked in, she was a hating ass bitch, to say the least.

"Barnes, what's going on, why don't you like Miko?" "Fuck that, she always trying to play the victim."

As soon as she said victim, I blacked out and threw a punch. I just remember them breaking up the fight and me leaving for the Greyhound bus the next day. Brit Brat was so sad to see me go, but I had to leave. She stood outside and waited for my cab with me.

"I am going to miss you like crazy." She cried. She really didn't want me to leave.

As soon as the cab got there and the driver placed my suitcase in the trunk, Brit Brat hugged me so tight, with tears rolling down her eyes. I hugged and kissed Trudy, and before getting in the cab, I looked back at Brit Brat and said, "I will always be your big sister, and I will always think of you, make sure you be good, okay." I cried the entire way to the bus station.

It was starting to feel like the Greyhound bus was my home. I rested my head on the cold glass window and imagined ways to make life better. There was so much time to think because the ride from Newburgh to Minnesota was thirty-six hours. I looked out the Greyhound window and tears rolled down my face. How many more homes? How many more heartbreaks? How many more bus rides? I was too young to be this exhausted.

When I arrived in Minnesota and was picked up by my Aunt Denna. She was tall, had a deep voice and always had a lit cigarette and a cold Pepsi.

"Hey Miko, you happy to be here."

"Yeah," it was all I could say. I wasn't trying to be rude.

We finally arrived at the house, and I immediately went in and greeted all my cousins. We had all grown up close together because our moms were both the black sheep of the family. My favorite cousin was Meech. He was just a few years younger than me, but we were still very close.

After I hugged my little cousins, he waved his hand. "Come on let's go out back."

There was a trailer home out back and all the bad kids hung out there. The moment I walked into the trailer, the smell of weed smacked me in the face. Another one of my cousins, who was tall and stalky, looked at me with a grin on his face.

"Aww damn, my bad, but you smoke, so it's all good." "Everyone listen up, this is my cousin."

All the guys jumped up and shared their names.

There was Mudd, he was black as night with white teeth, and he was cute.

There was Smiley, he was tall, wore braces, and from the looks of it, he had money and lots of it.

Then there was Pat and Mann-Mann, they were cousins and I found out they were the ones who got most of the girls. They created the clique, Deuces, who did not get along with the Selby side guys.

Pat walked up to me and said, "Man, you're beautiful."

"Thanks, can I hit the weed though?" I responded with attitude, and everyone laughed.

"Okay, I see you playing hard to get." He laughed.

I was not playing, I hated men who thought too highly of themselves. Not to mention, I was still with Dream.

Later that night, my sister came home. It had been years since she left Newburgh, so I was overwhelmed with excitement to see her and my new baby nephew. Samara was now sixteen years old, and she had become a teen mom. We hugged the moment she walked through the door, and she passed me my nephew. Kaydrim was so cute and chunky. He had the smoothest skin I had ever felt, and he was what most people would consider high-yellow. I was so excited to be a young aunty; I held him all night.

The next morning, I walked to the pay phone to call Dream. I missed him so much. Day after day, I would start my morning by walking to that pay phone to call him. Minnesota was so boring, and I missed Newburgh and my friends so much. All my old friends from Minnesota were long gone. After talking to Dream, I continued my day as usual. I needed to find something to do with my time because doing the same thing day after day was becoming mundane.

Later that day, I was sitting on the front porch and a young boy with a flannel shirt and a big smile came walking up to the screen door.

"May I help you?"

"Yeah, I think my dad is here?"

"Who is your dad?"

"Allen, he has been staying here." "Well, he isn't here."

"Damn, sweetie you ain't got to be like that." "Like what? Your dad isn't here."

"Okay, well is Meech here?" "No, he is at school."

"Okay well fuck it, can I wait here for one of them."

He was irritating but he also had a nice smile, so I opened the screen door for him.

"You must be the pretty cousin everyone is talking about." "Yeah, I guess." I sucked my lips and rolled my eyes. "What's your name?" He asked.

"Sumiko but you can call me Miko." "Sumiko, that's dope."

" Boy, you are asking all these questions, what's your name and how old are you?"

He looked young, but he acted like a grown man.

"My name is Louis and I'm thirteen years old, almost fourteen." "Wow, you're just a kid!"

"Sweetie, I am not a little boy, I do grown man shit."

He and I laughed and that was the start of many visits and conversations with Louis. Although I could tell he liked me, he was way too young for me. All I saw was a kid. However, I was beyond bored and lonely, so I engaged in conversation with him.

Once I was back in school, I met a few friends and we started hanging out often. I even got a job at McDonald's, and it helped with me being bored. I lived in that place. If they needed extra help, I was there. It worked out well because I needed to support myself and there was nothing else to do. After a while of living in Minnesota, I realized I still had not heard from my mother. I did some digging and come to find out that she'd moved to Delhi New York, to leave Omar. Apparently, she was finally fed up, and I was too excited to hear this. Deep down inside, I thought that there was hope for our relationship. I started to feel better inside knowing that my mother had left Omar. Reconnecting with my mom and siblings became my number one priority, so I started saving my money so I could buy a bus ticket to Delhi.

Unfortunately, against my better judgment, I loaned my aunt all the money I had saved so she could pay her bills on time. When I asked her for my money so I could buy some clothes, she flipped out and physically attacked me. To say I was shocked is an understatement. How are you getting mad at me about my money? In one swift move, I dodged a blow from her and ran out of that house to the pay phone. Some older guy had given me his number a few days ago and I decided to call him because I knew he liked me. I knew he would be willing to pay for my ticket home just in exchange to see me. He bought my ticket, and there I was back on the Greyhound … my second home.

What took my power - Feeling hopeless
Truth, I needed to accept - I was not okay

Everyone on this earth will feel defeated at some point in their lives. Feeling hopeless and defeated is one of the darkest spaces to be in. It's one of those feelings that make you feel like you have no power at all. When you experience challenge after challenge, disappointment after disappointment, you tend to stand down because you feel defeated. I know through reading scripture that God tells us that we should never stand down because He gave us the strength to overcome the toughest battles.

We must learn ways to overcome feelings of defeat because it takes away from our power. It's hard to focus on school when you're worried about where you're going to sleep that night. It's hard to keep your head up when you are surrounded by darkness. It's hard to love yourself when all you have received is hate and abuse from others. Overcoming feelings of hopelessness is going to be hard if you don't believe in the possibility of something greater. Many people overcome some of the most severe tragedies that cause them unbearable pain, but they still go on to live meaningful lives. I want to be clear; we have the power within us to do the same thing.

Tips on how to overcome hopelessness

Value your situation for what it is: Whether you're living in an apartment, or your own house, make sure you value it. Take care of it and make it feel like home. There are so many people in this world who do not have housing. You may not have the parents you wanted, the car you want, or the job you want, but if you start to compare and compete, you will never measure up to those standards. Value your current situation because it could always be worse.

Understand that things get greater, later: A big part of hopelessness is believing that things will not get better. The hopeless mindset makes us unmotivated and uninterested in life. For a lack of better words, it makes us give up and no longer try to be better. Some of us develop suicidal thoughts and some people feel so hopeless that they actually follow through with those thoughts. You must understand that time changes everything and if you put in the work, it can get greater, later.

Understand that you are not alone: When I was younger, and for most of my adult life, I felt alone. I mean, this statement is partially true, because I was alone. Now, I understand that there is always someone going through something similar and that I must reach out. There is always God, support groups, and crisis centers if I want support.

Practice Gratitude: Gratitude is beneficial for many reasons. For one, it makes you humble, and you do not become a person of pity or selfishness. It decreases worry, and it allows you to view your situation from a place of hope. Purchase a journal and use it as a place to share your gratitude. This will help you when you start to feel hopeless or defeated.

— 6 —

Acceptance

When I got back to Newburgh, I had no plan for housing, and I had no hope. I decided that I would spend the night wherever I could. Relying on myself to survive had long become the norm for me. Dream had an older sister who had her own place and I figured I could spend the night there as much as possible. I was going to make it happen the best I could.

When we first moved to Newburgh, I was quiet, shy, and didn't go out much. This time around, I was much different. In my mind, there was no need to be conservative. There was no hope left for me, so I needed to live my life to what I deemed was the fullest, which was basically not caring! Loud, obnoxious, and audacious were the new words to describe who I'd become. I no longer cared about being a good person, or even completing high school. All I wanted was to have fun and be happy. I'd officially become a product of my environment. The people, the places, and the things happening in my neighborhood began to shape me. Somewhere along my journey, I detoured and decided to take the path of self-destruction, not realizing just how bad that decision was until a lot of damage had been done. My town was surrounded by broken people. The woman I am now understands the power of people, places, and things, but not back then. I was foolish enough to believe that I was in control. If I was smart enough, I would have stayed in Minnesota because even though there was drama, it was a much better environment.

There were seven girls I hung out with every day, and the neighborhood named us the "Buck em" chicks. They named us this because I was always running my mouth and encouraging my girls to stand up for themselves. It was the first time I felt like I belonged. They treated me normal. They didn't care about my mom being a crackhead, or me being homeless. I was living on my own in the streets at fifteen-years-old. It didn't take me long at all to learn ways to make it look like I was okay. Looking back, I honestly don't know how little ol' me survived it all.

In my hopeless state, I thought it was cool to smoke weed, engage in violence, and be reckless. For food, I went to my friends' houses, and I also wore their clothes. Some days I went hungry, but I always found a way. My brothers were near, but I never could bring myself to tell them just how bad things really were. They thought I was living with a friend and that everything was good because that's what I told them.

All my friends came from loving homes, so inside, I felt inferior to them. There was Eb who was much older and was a neighbor to Diane. Diane was the second oldest of the crew. Then it was me, Ada, Gia, Malina, and Maria.

Eb, Diane's neighbor, was nineteen. Her mother was a crack addict and she lived with her aunt and uncle who were big-time drug dealers in the neighborhood. She was short, dark-skinned, and everyone called her "thick". She kept her hair and her nails done and she dressed nice. She talked to us about the neighborhood gossip. She also sold drugs for her uncle.

Then there was Diane who lived downstairs from Eb. They were like family. Diane was a straight-up gold digger. She acted much older than sixteen years old. Her parents allowed her to spend the night at her boyfriend's house and smoke weed. She was a light-skinned Puerto Rican who dressed nice and kept her nails done.

Then there was Maria. She lived with her older sister and grandmother. Her mother was an alcoholic. Although she was Honduran, she loved and appreciated black culture so we would often forget she wasn't black. She was skinny and tall, always dressed to the nines, and stayed covered in jewelry.

Malina was also Puerto Rican. She had dark hair and a pointy nose. She was beautiful. Ada was also Puerto Rican. Her demeanor and the way she carried herself was cool as hell. Her mother was decent, and she was well taken care of.

Gia was an only child, and she was spoiled. She had both of her parents and they made sure to meet her needs. She had a bunkbed, there was a fridge full of food and there were clean towels. I was always impressed by a house with clean towels because we never kept clean towels. Her mother washed and folded her clothes and left lunch money out for school. I used to love spending the night at her house. Gia also enjoyed me staying the night because she had no siblings. Her parents eventually allowed me to move into their home. They talked to my mom over the phone, and she of course agreed to let me stay there.

We were good kids, but still living before our time. We exhibited the same behavior we saw in our environment. It was normal for kids to smoke weed, have sex, and drink alcohol. It was normal for kids to sell drugs and drive fancy cars. It was exciting to see people fight. Young women were pregnant, and the neighborhood was crowded with dysfunction. I honestly did the best I could to survive, but even to this day, that period had a serious impact on my life. I will never forget the time I spent with my girls; it was some of the saddest, but greatest moments in my life.

I remember falling in love with weed. It made me forget about my problems and changed my overall mood. Eb also gave us alcohol sometimes. She shared stories about sleeping with other people's men and we were all interested in the drama. We sat on Diane and Eb's stoop until nighttime gossiping and smoking. `

I woke up the next morning to Gia yelling and crying. She was talking to the downstairs neighbor, Stanley.

"Nah, fuck him, I'm burning all this shit".

I came downstairs to Gia burning letters Gotti had written her. Usher's song let it burn was playing in the background. Looking back, that moment makes me laugh, but back then, Gia was really hurt. As much as I loved men, I hated them. I only knew two stand-up guys, the rest of the men were cheaters and abusers.

"Girl, fuck him, you're too good for him anyways!" I reminded her.

Acceptance

Seeing men have power over a woman like that disgusted me. It reminded me of my mom and Omar and that was triggering.

My friends and I were so young dealing with things we had no business dealing with. We thought we were in love. We all wanted to be loved. I literally believed back then that Dream and I would die together, so I understood why she was acting a fool.

We always met up at Diane and Eb's porch because their parents were cool. We smoked weed before and after school. Sometimes, we would even leave school to smoke. There was nothing in me that was interested in school back then. And even now I still remember that feeling of hunger in my stomach. I didn't even have a few dollars for a sandwich.

After moving in with Gia and her parents, they tried to love me, but I was such a discouraged child that I acted out. They eventually blamed me for Gia no longer being on the honor roll. I was pissed because if anything, it was Gotti that had her messing up in school, not me. This caused me to resent Gia since I felt she didn't stick up for me and allowed her parents to think that I was a bad influence.

"You should come work with me at Dairy Cone," Maria suggested one afternoon.

I shrugged, "Tell your manager to hire me."

It was Maria who made me love working. She worked hard when she was there, and she knew how to do her job. She had a good work ethic. Soon, we all ended up working at Dairy Cone. It was a small ice cream shop owned by a husband and wife. The wife was a mean old lady, but the husband was sweet. We called him Boss. He was old too, but he worked hard. I loved getting money so I could buy clothes and shoes. My self-esteem was building, while simultaneously still crumbling. Dream was riding around town with some white girl who drove a 2-door sports car. I couldn't compete with that. It was another reminder that I was broke. This killed my confidence and it made me feel inferior.

Even still, I never stopped being feisty and bold, and I walked around with my head held high. I owned rooms back then, but in a negative way. I thought it was cool being high at school and falling asleep in class. In my mind, it was cool being able to do what I wanted to do and acting tough. My mouth spewed venom to whomever, whenever. I was even disrespectful to my elders, especially if they disrespected me; I wasn't having it!

I was upstairs high and listening to music when Gia came running through the door.

"Girl, put your stuff on, Zuri is outside," she blurted.

Zuri was a girl I had punched the night before because I lost my temper.

I got up, changed my clothes, took off my earrings and tied my hair up. Once I stepped outside, I was surrounded by a crowd that had gathered to watch us fight. The truth is, I hated fighting, but I had something to prove. As soon as I stepped on the road, we fought. At this point, I was always getting into a fight and doing terribly in school. I was also about to be homeless again. Dream had made me miss curfew and Gia's parents told me I had to leave. They didn't care where I went that night because they were so angry. I remember walking around that entire night. I was only fifteen years old; anything could have happened to me. My grandmother lived around the corner, but I barely knew her, so I didn't go there. And although I had uncles and aunts in Newburgh, I hardly knew them either, so there I was, alone. I walked across town to my brother's baby mom's house because I spent the night there sometime. As soon as I walked in, I went to my nephew's room.

"Sumiko, can't nobody spend the night, I am missing a thousand dollars," she said.

Instead of being vulnerable and telling her I didn't have anywhere to go, I chose to just leave because I knew she was angry. I ended up walking around and hanging out with the drug dealers until morning came. Once 8 am hit, I went to Gia's to eat and get some rest. Her parents worked during the day, and she let me in while she went to school. It felt like I was always getting the short end of the stick in life, I was literally always going through something. And because I was hurt, I projected my anger onto everyone I met. People around town knew I would act crazy and cuss someone out in a minute if I felt threatened or disrespected. My apathetic behavior was for anyone and anything because I felt like I was doomed no matter what.

Once I started to self-sabotage, I did it in every way. First, the self-harm, then the suicide attempts, and that led me into promiscuity, and ultimately dropping out of school. Once I gave up on school, I gave up on everything! I had aspired to be a high school graduate, so once I made the choice to drop out of school, I felt even more powerless. It was something that hurt me to my core, and the only thing I could think of was going back to Minnesota. It was a humbling experience to watch my peers walk across that stage. On top of watching my peers graduate without me, more bullshit was headed my way. I woke up the next morning to some more devastating news.

"Yo, meet me at Diane's right now!" Malina shouted. "What's going on?" Her tone instantly made me nervous.

"Yo your brother is on the front page of the newspaper, they are saying he killed someone!"

"I'm on my way."

We all met up at Diane's, and then we walked to the Jamaican spot to buy some weed.

"Yo, this shit is crazy!"

"Yeah, I just hope this is not true."

We sat on the porch gossiping about everything. Diane's mother brought me the cordless phone and to my surprise, it was Tony. We all huddled up to hear what he had to say.

"What's going on?" I asked, hoping that the news was wrong.

"You see the newspaper, I gotta turn myself in." He had no emotion.

"Oh, my God, why!" I started screaming and crying, I was just getting close to him.

"I love you and don't worry, everything is going to work out. I'm about to come to see you before I leave."

Depression overtook me for days because I knew deep down inside that things were not going to be okay. In fact, things turned out to be even more damaging than I imagined. Tony pled guilty to murder and served five years in prison. He wrote me while he was there, but I was too unstable to keep in touch with him. When he came home, I talked to him on the phone because Gia had seen him and called me. He told me that he was on the run for a parole violation and that he would die before he returned to prison. Tony was murdered by police the next day. I would never see my brother again, and I had no choice but to accept my reality for what it was.

It soon became clear to me that if I did not change my surroundings, I would end up like the older people in my neighborhood who were strung out on drugs or in jail for doing something crazy. Newburgh was full of darkness, and I could finally see that. Not to mention that I was tired of Dream hurting me and I needed to do something; the only thing I knew how to do was leave. I called my sister and she bought me a bus ticket back to Minnesota. It had been a while since I rode in my second home, but there I was again, back like I never left.

What took my power- Being surrounded by darkness Truth, I needed to accept- I had to leave my friends to save myself

The environment that I was raised in didn't give me the language I needed to understand myself. Of course, being young and lacking real-life experience also played a part. Everyone in my neighborhood called me crazy, and I hated that. Now, my communication skills are much better, and I know now that I wasn't crazy, I was struggling with depression and anxiety.

Looking back, I was doing my best to survive. It's still hard to believe that I endured such pain, but that is my truth. I was a high school dropout; no job, no stable home, no plan for my future and no guidance; worst of all, I was hopeless. It was in that moment that I contemplated taking my own life once more, but really following through with it. Instead, however, I did what I knew best in that moment, I prayed.

Tips on how to cope with negative people, places, and things: Remove unhealthy people from your life: It was hard for me to walk away from people that I loved. I grew up with the thought that love meant that you stay. I did not know what a healthy relationship was. You must understand that if you continue to allow unhealthy people to remain in your life, they will continue to take your power and that's the truth.

Spend as much time as possible in healthy spaces: The older I get, the more I realize that I cannot have peace in spaces that are full of chaos. Whether it's a toxic work environment, home environment, school environment, club etc, you must leave those spaces, or your spirit will pay the price. An unhealthy space can destroy the healthiest person over time. If you are currently in negative spaces, change your environment.

Never give power to anything that does not serve you: When I was young, I defended myself constantly. My goal was to always make people understand who I was. I wanted to prove something. I was always giving my power away to things that did not serve me. You must become wise enough to understand the difference between things that are meant to help you and things that were meant to destroy you. Trauma makes it difficult to recognize safety, but you must work on this issue.

— 7 —

Shame and Guilt

There I was, at eighteen years old, headed back to St. Paul, Minnesota. And I still didn't have a home. There was no job waiting for me and no plan for my life. On the inside, I felt constant turmoil. As I laid my head on the Greyhound bus window, I thought about life and tried to figure out how I could create a better one for myself. It felt like I was always struggling; no stability, no direction, no love, and worst of all – no family. At this point, I was just tired of being sick and tired. What seemed to be so basic, I lacked, and that took away from my ability to feel empowered.

These truths shook my world, but I could cope with them better if I denied them.

I got off on University Avenue in St. Paul and hopped on the 64-city bus to my sister's house, and of course, no one was there to pick me up. It was just another reminder that I was out here on my own. I arrived at my sister's front door and the smell of weed smoke smacked me in the face. I knocked on the door and one of my sister's ghetto-ass friends opened the door. She was loud and hyper.

"Oh, my God, your little sister is too cute."

People always commented on my beauty, but all I saw was imperfection and so I hated compliments, they always made me feel uncomfortable. "Hey," was my response. I walked past her reaching for my nephews.

My sister and I did not greet each other with a hug, we just said hi. We didn't know how to love each other. Suzie was now twenty years old and had two sons; ages one and three years old. I spent a lot of time watching my nephews. They were, and still are, my world. My sister was young, and so of course she was not perfect. We smoked weed and hung out with the kids, but she loved and took care of her kids. My nephew's dad's brother was at my sister's when I arrived in St. Paul, and he and I would ultimately end up with a child together. Yea, you heard me right. Our kids became cousins on both sides. And yes, I know that's pretty ratchet.

Jalil was about 5 ft 9, and honestly ugly as hell. He was quiet and smoked weed all day every day, which is why we started hanging out. I was using him to get high. Looking back, he definitely groomed me. He was six years older than me and used my loneliness and vulnerability to his advantage. I was so bored when I moved to St. Paul that he became my comfort. I missed my friends back home, but there was no longer anything there for me. I felt so lonely, and even though I was surrounded by people, these were not "my people". I thought that Dream and Buck 'Em would be a part of my life forever. Truth is, nothing is forever. And although it was one of the happiest moments in my life, that's all it was, a moment. I had so much fun with this group of girls and Newburgh was where my heart was. I tried my hardest to move forward, but it was so hard.

I walked to the corner store a lot just to become familiar with my new home. It was something about moving back and forth between states that made me feel lost inside. It was about 90 degrees, and I was walking back from the corner store. I heard a car coming toward me blasting some loud music, it was Jalil.

"Can I give you a ride?"

"Yeah, it's hot as hell!" I hopped in the car and hit the blunt. His car did not have AC, so we rode with the windows down for air.

"So, don't you have a girl?" I asked because he'd been doing a lot of flirting since I met him.

"You know, I live with my baby's mom." He said.

He had a three-year-old son who had been diagnosed with Autism and he lived with the mother of his son. He claimed that they were breaking up soon. "See you later," he pulled off music blasting.

As soon as I walked through the door, my sister started lecturing me.

"Girl, I don't know why you hang out with him, you know his baby mom is going to start thinking something."

"I do not give a fuck about that chick, Jalil and I do not have anything going on!"

"Okay, I just don't want any problems, did you get the blunts?". "Yeah."

As the days passed, Jalil eventually moved out of his baby mom's house and started living with my sister and me. We watched movies and smoked blunts all day. There were times when he lusted over me so bad that he would just sit on the couch and stare at me. I didn't like him the way he liked me, but I tolerated his company.

Instead of finding my own friends, I just hung out with my sister's friends. Across the street in the same complex was a girl named Tasha, she was pretty ghetto, and as much as I hate this word, I'm telling you, this girl put the G in ghetto. She had two bad ass kids who cursed everyone out. I became close to her, though because I accepted people for who they were. Even though we were different, we were the same.

"So, what is it like in Newburgh? You sound just like them people from New York," Tasha laughed.

People always questioned if I was really from New York because they had never heard of Newburgh, and that was irritating.

"It's cool, there's always something to do and the stores are open all night."

"So, you know my cousin likes you, right?" "Who, Jalil? Doesn't he have a girl?"

"Man fuck that bitch! Nah, I'm just kidding, shit y'all both my friends now."

We both giggled because she was friends with Jalil's girl.

I eventually gave in to Jalil and I started having a relationship with him. My sister was right, his baby's mom and her friends pulled up to my sister's house and tried to jump me. I was able to run into the house before they got to me. My sister was pissed and wanted me to leave her house.

"I told you that this was going to happen!"

"Man, you're my big sister, you should have my back."

"I can't have your back when your bringing drama to my house and I have two babies, you need to find somewhere else to live!"

Quickly, I walked away from her so she couldn't see my tears. There was nowhere for me to go. I called up an older man who liked me and asked if he could pick me up. He agreed. I said goodbye to my nephews and my sister. I went back to grab my bag because I had no plans on coming back. I didn't know where I was going, but I was too stubborn to stay.

"Where are you going?" She looked worried because she knew I didn't have anywhere to go.

"I will be staying with my friend until I find somewhere to live."

"You don't have to leave."

"I know."

I walked out of the door. I hopped in the car and broke down crying. The older guy's name was Ben, he was African and talked with an accent. He had a nice car and a good job. He liked me but I didn't like him, he was healthy but I wasn't attracted to that. To be honest, I used Ben for the things he did for me. During the car ride to his house, he broke the silence.

"Why are you crying?"

"My sister just kicked me out."

"Why don't you enroll in Job Corps? They will help you get a trade, and you can live there. Don't cry, I will take you there tomorrow to get signed up."

The next morning, he drove me to Job Corps. I signed up and that's where I lived for the next 6 months. Of course, Job Corps was a struggle, but for the first time in my life, I did not give up. I was almost kicked out several times for my behavior, but I turned it around because I finally found something to care about. I got my

G.E.D and a certificate in culinary arts. I got to wear a cap and gown which made me feel a little better about dropping out of high school. I felt a little sad that my mother was not there cheering me on, but I kept my head up.

After I completed Job Corps, I decided to get my own place so my sister could stop putting me out of her house. I was over being put out on the streets. Not having a place to call home took so much power from me and having my own could help make it better.

My first apartment

I was working part-time at Burger King which was enough to afford my own place back then. My first apartment was a small one-bedroom off Payne Avenue for 400 dollars a month. I remember how good it felt to sign my first lease. My sister gave me her old furniture from the basement, and I bought a bed and some other house décor and moved in right away. I didn't stop cleaning and decorating until I felt that everything was perfect. Having my own place made me so happy. It made me feel good about myself. There was purple and green décor in my bathroom, and I was finally able to purchase the black lamp I always wanted. To ensure I could cover my bills and live comfortably, I picked up more hours and started receiving bigger checks. Unfortunately, I had to walk back and forth to work most of the time which was irritating, but I did it until I got fed up with it. Then, I started saving money for a car and finally bought one.

Parenthood

When I decided to have my first child, I had no idea how much of my power it would take to raise a healthy child. I was young, dumb, and not ready to be anyone's mother. In my mind, I felt having a child would be easy because I would be the exact opposite of my mother. I also thought that I was prepared because I had a place to live, a car, and an income. The truth is, I was too young to even realize that parenting was much more than that. What I learned is that parenting includes preparation, two healthy parents, and real-life experience.

My introduction to motherhood started off all wrong, and thus it was hard. I was with a man who didn't love me, and he was not prepared to take care of a child. Also, because I wasn't planning on getting pregnant, I was still out on the streets living recklessly.

One evening, Meech, my favorite cousin, and I were out joy-riding around. The weather was perfect for blasting music while riding with the windows down to enjoy the breeze.

"Aye pull over, there goes Louis. Let's see what this lil dude is up to," Meech said, pointing.

I put on the turn signal and made a right into the parking lot of a local store and turned down the radio.

Meech smiled, "Aye Louis, what's up dude?"

As I looked over, I caught eye contact with this dude who looked as if he had seen the woman of his dreams. He totally ignored Meech and asked me a question instead.

"Is this your cousin from New York?"

Before I could even respond, he continued, "Yes, it is, you remember me? Girl, I have been wishing to God, that I could see you again."

He jumped in the back seat of my car, and we talked for what seemed like hours. Over the next few months, we kicked it often. He would come to ring my doorbell and smoke with me. He was always there, but I didn't take him seriously, he was still just a kid to me and just another nigga trying to have sex with me. He was tall, brown-skin, handsome, and had a pretty smile. After kicking it with Louis for New Year's Eve, I woke up feeling sick.

In early 2004, I remember feeling sick, but this was a different kind of sickness. Jalil and I had been intimate, but I honestly hadn't thought anything else about that time I spent with him. However, now my chest was hurting whenever I ran up the stairs and I couldn't eat. My period was also late, and although I dreaded the mere thought of it, I knew deep down there was a chance I could be pregnant. Later that day, I took the pregnancy test, and sure enough, I was pregnant.

Although I was afraid as ever, at that moment, I knew I was keeping this child. Jalil was still with Dricka, but I thought that having his child would make him choose me. I was naïve enough to believe that this baby would make Jalil leave his girl and get back with me. Excitement overtook me and I couldn't wait to tell him that I was pregnant.

Grabbing my phone, I called Jalil over and the moment he walked into my apartment, I told him that I was pregnant. His reaction wasn't what I had expected, however. Instead of hugging me and being happy, this fool looked me right in my eyes and asked, "Are you sure this is my baby?"

"Of course, this is your baby. You're the only person I've been having sex with!" I yelled.

Frustration overwhelmed me. I was angry and hurt and could not believe he was asking me this. I wasn't the kind of girl to sleep around and in my mind, he was calling me a hoe.

"So, do you want me to keep this baby?" I asked him.

"Of course, you should have kept the first baby, why would I not want my baby? I have to go, Drika is expecting me home for dinner."

I took a step back, threw up my hands, and yelled, "Drika! Fuck her! You should be staying with me tonight, I'm pregnant with your baby!"

His shoulders dropped and he shook his head as if he was exhausted, "I have to go. I will come over in the morning when she goes to work."

A river of tears fell out of nowhere as I pleaded, "Please stay with me! Please don't leave me tonight, I need you!"

After pushing me off him, he turned around and walked out the front door. That day, he took a little piece of my heart when he walked out that door. It felt like I was re-living the moment when I needed my mother most and she walked out on me. In tears and complete agony, I stretched out on the couch, curled up in a ball, and bawled. It was more than evident that I was searching for love in the wrong place.

Drowning in my sorrows had to end abruptly because someone rang my doorbell a couple of hours later. Quickly, I wiped my tears and rushed over to the window to see who it was. Louis gave me a huge grin when he saw me peeping. As soon as he entered my apartment, I asked him to go into the bathroom and look at the sink. Disappointment covered his face as he solemnly made his way back to the living room, but he still mustered up a smile and congratulated me. Although he was clearly upset, he knew he really had no place to have an opinion on my life because he, and I, were just good friends. I told him about Jalil's reaction and how upset I was. He laid with me, wiped my tears, and rubbed my stomach until I fell asleep. He was so sweet to me, and I was too busy chasing a man that did not want me. Healthy love was just unheard of for me back then.

Being pregnant with Jalil's child canceled any plans of me ever moving back to Newburgh. I was officially stuck in Minnesota. However, finding out I was pregnant did give me something positive to focus on. It gave me a reason to care about life.

My mom's addiction reached one of its highest peaks when I was pregnant with my first child.

I was living in Minnesota and my mother and younger siblings were back living in Newburgh.

As crazy as it may sound, being pregnant made me want to reconnect with my mother and little sisters so much. I needed my mom so badly and I was still naive and hoped that things would be different. After thinking of a plan that would work for me and Jalil, I was headed back to Newburgh to visit and reconnect with my family.

I had gained a good friend since moving back to Minnesota,

her name is Rose. She was as loyal as they came. She was loud, an Aquarius just like me, and she was my twin flame. She was the only person I trusted with my house keys, so I called her up to see if she could watch over my apartment while I was away.

"Hey girl, what are you doing?" "Nothing, sitting here, bored."

"So, I decided to go to Newburgh for a few months to see my mom and sisters, I need you to pay my rent and check on my place every now and then."

"Okay, you know I got you, when are you leaving?" "Next week, I will give you my keys tonight." "Okay when I come outside, I will grab them".

As I drove to the Greyhound bus station, tears started to fall, I always cried when I was by myself because I was so unhappy. This time, I was crying because I didn't know what to expect from my mother. My home girl Gia who was a part of the group I was in while living in Newburgh was picking me up from the bus station where I now stood filled with mixed emotions. I heard someone yelling and of course, it was Gia.

"Hey preggo."

"Bitch, here you go." We both laughed.

"Girl, Dream was like yo, tell your girl to holla when she gets here." I was like "Boy, just because yo name is Holla, doesn't mean my girl wants to Holla, she is pregnant by another man, so leave my friend alone."

"Girl, that's my friend I'm ma go see him." Our conversation went from laughter to silence and then Gia broke the ice.

"Girl, I don't know how to tell you this, but yo mother looks really bad."

"Girl, how bad could it be? She has been using drugs my entire life," I said laughing. We rode in silence until we reached my mother's house.

"Girl, call me once you get settled." "Okay."

I looked up and there was a 3-story brick building that didn't look too bad for Newburgh. I knocked on the door and my mother opened it.

"Hey baby."

The moment I saw her shriveled face, tears immediately rolled down my eyes and I felt sick to my stomach. Gia was right. She looked so bad. It literally looked as though she was skin and bones, and her hair had almost completely fallen out. She looked completely strung out.

"Why are you crying?" She looked confused, but also ready to continue getting high.

"What do you mean, look at you, look at this house, you got my little sisters fucked up!"

My little sisters stood in the corner waiting for me to say hi. The house was filthy and could have been abandoned.

"Hey you guys." I hugged them and they looked happy to see me, but also mad because I was talking about their home. I walked into the first bedroom and lay down.

Omar's yelling and screaming, calling my little sisters bitches, is what woke me out of my slumber. I could not believe that my mother allowed him to come over knowing I was visiting. Of course, I woke up and immediately ran into the living room.

"How can you call your own daughter bitches?"

"Shut the fuck up, these are my kids!" He was standing over top of me and I blacked out. I grabbed the empty 40-ounce bottle sitting on the table and busted him right in the head. Glass shattered, and everyone was yelling and screaming. He had blood coming down his head, and at that moment, he pushed me and my pregnant belly against the wall and ran into the bathroom. My mom of course ran to his rescue.

"What the hell is going on?"

"I am calling the police, he just pushed me, and I'm seven months pregnant!". I ran down the stairs to wait for the police. The police pulled up, and my sister Kay came outside from next door and watched.

"What's going on?" One of the two officers asked, the other one standing with his hand on his gun.

My mother and Omar ran down the stairs. The police immediately tried to handcuff Omar until my mother stopped them and asked, "Why are you arresting him? He is the one bleeding!"

"You stupid bitch! I literally hate you, how can you defend him, I am pregnant! I hope you die!" I was screaming and crying. My older sister on my father's side happened to come outside. She lived with our great-grandmother whose house was right next door. She ran over and hugged me.

"You're okay Miko, I will grab your things you're coming to stay with us." She walked me into the house, and I rested for hours. I woke up to some food and my sister talking. "Ya mother is so fucked up for that, I'm glad you hit him with that bottle. My sister had that deep New York accent, and I loved the way she talked.

"Yeah, I am over it. I am just focused on my little Ladybug". I was so happy to be having a girl!

Some of you may wonder why I went back. I went back because I still had some hope that things could be different. My mother's love was something I wanted and needed, and so I went back. Even though I was still angry, and I was depressed. I was also still in denial, and I had not reached the point of acceptance. I needed to accept the fact that my mother was not capable of loving me. Also, I had to accept the fact that this was my mother's husband and she had chosen him over me. The more I begged her to put me first, the harder it was for me to heal. It was time for me to let it go. The hurt and pain they'd caused me was showing up in my relationships and it would ultimately impact me as a mother. My mom still battles with drugs today, but it does not upset me anymore. I have accepted the fact that my mother is sick and me being upset can't change that.

I flew back to Minnesota early August after staying with my sister for the rest of the time I was in Newburgh. It was years before I saw my mother again. On August 19th, 2005, there I was at Children's hospital giving birth to my first child, Ladybug. She came out with a head full of hair and big bright eyes. I was exhausted, but I still leaned my face against hers and that was the start of my journey as a mother.

What took my power - Feeling like a failure
Truth, I needed to accept - I had made a lot of bad choices

As much as I wanted to be a good person and a good parent, I had to admit to myself that I just didn't have the skills or knowledge to do so. I caused myself, others, and my kids a lot of traumas and I had to forgive myself for that. I allowed my children to witness my abuse and I projected my fears onto them. Men were allowed to hurt me, and I could not find peace. To ignore my reality, I spent many years in denial about who I was. I had to open my eyes and really see myself for who I was. Of course, Ladybug experienced a lot more traumas because she was my first child. She went through all my ups and downs and suffered because of my choices. I could tell that my brokenness had impacted her and that hurts me to my core.

A part of me blamed myself because I knew that she had a traumatic childhood, but the other part of me showed myself grace because I was doing the best I could. I heard someone say that hurt people have hurt children, who have hurt children and that was my truth. I was able to get through my daughter's adolescent years by reminding myself that I am not perfect. I was also willing to do whatever it took to get my daughter back on track. At one point, I was more concerned about what people would think about my parenting and less about why my daughter was having behavioral problems at school. Accepting the fact that my daughter was struggling in school, and she might be transferred to a behavioral school was hard for me. However, it was her journey and I had to stop trying to control that. Being an authoritative parent, I don't believe, worked for my daughter. She already had an absent father, so she needed me to be more nurturing. She needed my love and my hugs. All three of my children needed a healthy mom. Shame made me feel stuck at times, and suicidal. There were so many days that I almost took my own life because I thought that this world would be better off without me. Everyone threw my bad choices in my face and shamed me, instead of helping me.

Tips on how to let go of shame and guilt

Love your child and apologize: A big part of letting go of the mistakes you make as a parent is admitting your wrongs. Most children are just looking for validation or a sincere apology. The moment you start making excuses or telling your children "I did the best I could," is the moment you hurt them all over again. Hear your children out and validate their feelings. Always tell your children you love them and give them hugs. I will be honest, hugging my children did not come natural to me because I didn't receive that kind of love. I had to recognize this and be intentional about hugging my children.

Be vulnerable: Speak your truth out loud and don't be afraid to share your story; even the most shameful parts of it. Writing this book and telling the world about my mistakes was not easy, but I was willing to be vulnerable so that others could understand me entirely, and not just parts of me. What people do with the information I've shared, even in this book, is on them. I am no longer a victim of shame.

Admit to your mistakes and forgive yourself: If the words of someone else can make you feel less about yourself, then you probably struggle with shame. You cannot walk in power if you are still punishing yourself for the mistakes you have made. Only you know who you are and why you have made the mistakes you have made. If you know that at the core of who you are lies a good person, then that is your truth; you're a good person. Own your mistakes and no one can ever make you feel ashamed of who you are. None of us are perfect, so forgive yourself for trying to be.

— 8 —

Lost and Found

By the time I was twenty-five years old, I was completely lost. I had been traveling down a dark path for a long time. My behavior and my thinking patterns were working against me. Multiple men had enjoyed access to my body without protection. My insides felt dead, and they poured into my everyday walk in life, from my dead-end jobs to my lifeless relationships. It frustrated me to no end because I knew I was better than this. I was abusing myself. Coping skills, boundaries, and self-love were non-existent when it came to my life. Honestly, I was checked out and operating on autopilot.

Once again,there I was by myself in this huge world trying to figure things out. There was more money going out than coming in which caused me to struggle to keep up with my bills. However, it was mostly because I was reckless with my money. I did everything I could to get money, and when I say everything, I mean EVERYTHING. I even had a short moment of trying to sell crack cocaine, because where I came from, it was an instant way to get money. It couldn't be too hard to bag up some crack and sell it.

To get my hands on it, I called up some of my male friends I knew through my sister. When I told the guy on the phone who I was and asked him if he would be able to get me some crack, he said yes. That same day, I picked up an 8 ball of crack and started reaching out to the people who I thought were using crack. I'll never forget meeting this woman who was at the bus stop. She was big, but she was dressed up nicely. I remember asking her if she did drugs; even though she did not look like the type to be strung out on drugs, it looks like she dabbled in drugs and so I asked her.

She followed me back to my house, and honestly, I didn't have my guard down with her. It was mainly because I've always trusted women. I've never really been in a situation with a woman where I didn't feel safe and so I invited her into my house. That day, I was extremely sick, so once she and I made it into my apartment, I was very tired. Not too long after we were in my place, she asked me if she could get the month of April on credit until she got paid. Being a rookie and not really knowing about the drug game, I said yes. She gave me her credit card for collateral and when I woke up the next morning, she was completely gone. I still had her card, but when I checked the balance, it said the card had been cancelled. I Immediately called my friend who issued the crack to me.

"Hey, this lady just ran off with of my drugs. She gave me her credit card, but the card is saying it's cancelled. What should I do?

There was silence on the other end before he let out a sigh and said, "Don't worry about it. We will get your money back."

And that's pretty much what we set out to do. I can't remember how or when I got it, but I had this person's address. We drove to her house and when we get there, I noticed she lived in some type of assisted living place.

"Wait, I think this is an old folks' home and they have security." "Man, Fuck security,we're here to get your money, don't worry about it."

I've always been fearless, and I've always hated someone taking advantage of me, I think the combination of both of those things led me to easily making an impulsive decision.

We got into the building, and I can't really recall the details, but I do remember we found her apartment. Shortly after we knocked on the door, she opened it and immediately screamed for help. More than being upset, I think I was hurt because I feel like she took advantage of a young woman who she clearly knew was a rookie. No real drug dealer will ever allow anyone to get credit unless they really know and trust them.

As she screamed for help, other tenants started coming out of their apartment doors full of concern. We ran out of that building so fast, I never got my money, and that was the end of me selling crack. It was a huge loss, but it was also a huge lesson. I learned that when you are involved in any kind of street transactions, there are really no rules. You enter into that lifestyle at your own risk, and you can live by it or die by it. I knew then that I was not really feeling that lifestyle because I'm not an evil person and I don't wanna have to put my hands on somebody or really harm somebody because they didn't pay me my money and so I was back to the drawing board.

Poverty puts you in survival mode which causes you to only think for the moment. I never understood how some people could have millions and then there was me, struggling to put five dollars of gas in my tank. This was one of the many reasons why I hated my life. At the time, I didn't know it, but I had developed a negative thinking pattern which in the end took away from my ability to solve problems. Further, it caused me to live with a victim mindset. Inside, I wanted to give up, but on the outside, I kept going.

There was now an eviction on my record, so I had no idea how I was going to get a new place. In my world, it was barrier after barrier and me constantly fighting for more. If me not being able to get good housing weren't bad enough, I also needed a car that was reliable. I can't stress enough how important it is to pay your bills and remain a law abiding citizen. I had a lot of risky behaviors; from riding around with drug dealers, to sleeping around with multiple men within months apart, to even using ecstasy pills occasionally. I was unaware of how to keep myself in safe spaces. As you grow, hopefully, you will learn from your experiences. If you continue to get results you don't want, you must change yourself because it's the only person you have power over.

I was desperate to find a way out

My cousin Quack had enrolled in college and started practicing Islam. He told me that college would pay me money while I went to school. Originally, I signed up just for the student loans. However, I eventually began to really want to become a college graduate. I was learning how to survive by any means, but I also wanted better. It's true what they say, "You have to want it". Thankfully, at that time, I was living in a one-bedroom apartment that was inexpensive and so paying the rent was not a stress for me. I went to school and paid my bills, and for the first time, I had real stability.

Of course, having my own place was not enough to keep me happy. My spirit needed to be filled in other ways. Jalil was still with Drika, and I was depressed. Even with things starting to get better for me, I wanted to give my apartment up and go back to Newburgh. However, I would soon receive some news that would keep me in Minnesota indefinitely.

I met Carter. He had the most beautiful eyes and beautiful white teeth I'd ever seen. Thankfully, he also didn't notice I was pregnant.

I was only four months at the time, and I was kind of scared to tell him on the spot, so I just responded quickly, and gave him my phone number. He called me as soon as I got home, and we made plans to see each other later that night. The moment I opened the door that night when he came by my place, I blurted out "I'm pregnant". He smiled and said that that was okay. He went on to say he was a father of two himself and his youngest child was nine months old.

While we kicked it that night, he smoked his blunt. I was pregnant and was no longer smoking at the time and so we just kind of chilled. Then, I remember us lying on my couch and falling asleep until the next morning. I really liked Carter, however, I found out soon after we started dating that he was still in a relationship with the mother of his children because she called my phone. She was a beautiful girl I went to high school with. A part of me really couldn't understand why he would be after anybody else when he had such a beautiful woman at home. I also think that's when I realized that no matter what you give a person or no matter how beautiful you are, the timing and commitment must be there, or he will seek more. I did not realize it at the time, but I was codependent as hell, and was always chasing a man.

One day, he told me that we needed to get a place further out because he wanted to be as far as way from his children's mother as possible. He told me they had broken up and I believed it. I did not give notice to my place, I just packed up and moved about thirty minutes away from the city to a place that I ended up paying almost triple the rent. So many people told me that I was making a mistake and that paying $400 in rent in my current state was not going to be easy to come by. However, I felt I needed to do what I thought was right for me at the time, and I decided that the move was a smart decision. In my mind, it would bring Carter and me closer. My best friend T, and his best friend Mitch helped me to move into my new place. I didn't necessarily realize it at the time, but Carter was using me for whatever he could get. He would ask me to borrow money, he would ask me to buy him things, he would ask me to babysit, and he drove my car more than I did. He would pretty much use me for anything that was beneficial to him. In return, as long as he spent time with me, I was okay with being used. Again, at that time in my life, I was still in a place of needing love to the point of desperation.

Soon, I got a better paying job to pay for the new apartment I had just rented, and I will never forget it. It was at a nursing home, and I was working as a dietary aide in the kitchen with some old white women who had been at the company for well over twenty years. I was coming in late, while under the influence of marijuana, and I just was not taking things seriously.

One day, Carter called me to tell me that he needed me to take him to do something. If I agreed to do it, I knew it would make me late for work, but I decided I was willing to be late to make sure that Carter got what he needed. When I got to work that day, the manager called me into her office. she was an African American woman and she looked right at me and told me that I could not be late again, or she would have to fire me.

As time went on, I was on time, but then there was a snowstorm and it caused me to have a flat tire. I was panicking on the inside because I didn't know how to change a tire and I didn't have anyone to call for a ride. You would think that Carter would have helped me, but he didn't answer the phone. I thought given the situation my manager would be understanding of the fact that it's a snowstorm and I had a flat tire. I finally arrived to work two hours late that day and again my manager called me in her office.

She looked me dead in the face and said, "Listen, I told you last time that I could no longer allow you to come in late. We have people here who are upset about this and feel that you're not a fit for the team. I hate to do this, but I have to let you go, you need to get your shit together so you can become a better woman for yourself."

I just sat there as a few tears rolled down my face. Then, I got up and left. I think it was in that moment that I realized that I was lost. I had no idea where I was going in life and how I would get there. Not only had I dropped out of college, I was also about to be homeless.

Soon, I could no longer pay the rent because it is so high, so I had to move out. I will never forget the fear I felt when I came home to an eviction letter. Toya came over to help me move my stuff out and I had to throw most of it away. It was hard and honestly, I felt like the biggest piece of shit that day. It was in that moment that I realized I was putting my daughter through the same things I had been through. Even still, I was too proud to ask for help because I could not take anyone putting me down. The mere thought of anyone doing that shattered me. I parked behind my aunt's house, and I held Ladybug until we fell asleep. That night, I fell asleep in tears because I knew she deserved better. She was only 6 months old. We slept in the car that night, but I woke up the next morning and went inside my aunt's house.

"Hey auntie."

"Hey Miko, what brings you by?"

"I was just in the neighborhood." I said and sat down. Before I knew it, I had fallen asleep with Ladybug sitting up on my lap. I was so tired.

Eventually, I broke down and went back to stay with my sister.

Minnesota in the winter was one of the coldest states known to man.

My sister didn't have any objections, she just said, "If you're going to be staying here, just make sure you help clean and pay something on the bills."

Everything was cool for a few weeks, but sooner than later, we were fighting and me and Ladybug were being put out. My sister was mean and cold, it was the only way she knew how to be.

"How could you put your niece out in the cold, that don't make any sense." Tears were rolling down my eyes. It was such an embarrassment and a shame for me to be homeless with a baby on my hip. After grabbing a few items, I loaded Ladybug in the car, thanking God that I at least had a car. I looked back at her in the car seat, and she was smiling at me. As much as I wanted to give up, I knew I couldn't because then I would be just like my mother. I humbled myself and called the local shelters.

As embarrassed as I was, I did what I had to do.

"Here is your room". I was placed in a room that had 2 bunk beds and there was a mother and her son on the other bunk. I did not want to talk, so I hurried and jumped in my bed, held Ladybug close, and fell asleep. I was never alone after having Ladybug, I always had her by my side.

The next day, I woke up and dropped her off to daycare. I was working at the bank which was one protective factor. I was very different from my co-workers. They came from love and money. We had very different problems. They were arguing with their parents about the car they wanted, and I was begging Jalil to babysit. I had mastered "being okay" when I needed to be. No matter where I went, I always seemed to be the one with the most chaos. I got off work, picked Ladybug up from daycare, and hung out with Tara (my best friend) for a little while. That night, I arrived at the shelter around 10 p.m. and decided to wash a load of clothes.

"Um you're not allowed to wash clothes this late," one of the staff workers said.

I was going through so much that this comment triggered something.

"Bitch, I will do whatever I want to do." She looked at me like she couldn't believe what I'd just said, then she turned and walked away.

I woke up to staff asking me to come to the office.

"Hey, we are so sorry, but you can't stay here anymore, we can't have you disrespecting our staff." I just sat there with Ladybug on my lap, A few tears dropped, but I did what I always did when I was being kicked out of a place, I left.

Looking back, of course all of this could have been prevented if I had known what boundaries were. I allowed a man to uproot me and my child's stability and that's my truth.

It was about ten degrees outside, and I had three large garbage bags. Just as I was walking out, snow started to fall. I looked up at the sky and I was all out of energy. I stopped right there and asked God for help. I drove around for hours and eventually ended up calling Jalil. I was always being saved by him. He was homeless as well, but a friend of his allowed us to stay in a spare bedroom. Based off the news I was about to receive, Jalil was the last person I should have been calling. I was getting ready to go out for my birthday and I received a call from my clinic.

"Hi, may I speak to Sumiko Knight." "This is she. How can I help you?".

"This is the nurse at Face-to-Face clinic, I was calling to let you know that you tested positive for Chlamydia and trichomoniasis."

"Okay thank you." I sat in that chair feeling ashamed, but then anger took over.

I drove straight to the block looking for Jalil and there he was sitting on the porch with his homeboys.

"Why the fuck are you giving me STD's?" He looked at me and

grabbed me by the throat, choking me until I could no longer speak.

"Shut the fuck up," he whispered the words like they were venom.

The moment he released my neck, I grabbed it choking and ran back to my car and immediately went to pick up my prescription. Mentally, I was in such a bad space back then, so much so, I still found myself back in bed with Jalil the same night. He even gave me Chlamydia again years later. Looking back, it makes no sense. I accepted how he treated me; I did not have the boundaries within myself to establish better treatment. I just yelled, cried, and repeated the cycle.

I allowed Jalil to break me down as a mother and a woman. Daily, I begged for his love. Dricka eventually left him, but in the end, I was the one who lost. He did help keep Ladybug while I worked. I paid all the bills so it was the least he could do. I was working ten to twelve hour shifts as a dishwasher. I came home wet every night, smelling like wild rice soup and beer. I did what I had to do to keep a place, a car, and some money in my pocket. Daily, I had to remind myself that hard work and consistency would pay off. There were times when I worked from three pm to three am washing dishes. My attire consisted of these huge pants with a button up white shirt and a chef's hat. I did not care, though, I needed a job, and I was willing to do whatever. One day, I was on the elevator with my manager and the guys who were supposed to be training me. Of course, the black dude said exactly what was on his mind.

"Damn, I have never seen someone look so good in this uniform. With all due respect young lady, you make it look good." Everyone agreed and smiled.

I was used to men saying and doing what they wanted for the most part, but it was those kinds of interactions that literally made me freeze. I just didn't care for the attention.

One night, I was training with a guy named Gaylord and Martinez. The first night was going well and then out of nowhere came the bullshit.

I was standing in front of the dishwasher just having a general conversation with Martinez.

"Hey, where did you work before this?" He asked me.

"I used to work at a bank, but I quit, due to wanting a better position at the bank. What kept me from getting the better position was not passing the background check so here I am," I smiled.

"Oh, what kind of panties do you wear?" He asked, as he proceeded to walk pass me and rub his penis on my butt.

My body began to shake as I started having a flashback of Omar's face. I was feeling all kinds of emotions, and although I didn't say anything, I ran straight to the supervisor.

I stood in the doorway of her office and as soon as she realized I was crying she jumped out of her chair.

"What's wrong? Please come have a seat."

"Martinez is asking me what kind of panties I wear, and he rubbed himself against me."

She immediately told me to go home for the night and she would address the situation right away.

I felt embarrassed, but I also wondered why men crossed my boundaries so much. Was I smiling too much, did I give off that kind of energy?

The next day, there was another awkward moment on the elevator. "Yo, you better not say anything to her, or your ass will get fired."

One of the guys said as they all laughed.

"That's not funny, that dude violated me, it's his own fault he got fired."

"Dudes been working here for five years and he has a family to feed. I'm just saying, did you have to tell on him, you couldn't just talk to him?'"

Gaylord was working with me that night, he grabbed me by the arm and took me off the elevator.

"Don't worry about them fools, you did what was right, but I won't lie, you're fine as hell!"

We both laughed, Gaylord and I had become close. He was my protector there. I also became close with the other guys.

I worked there for a few years, I would come home smelling like food, shirt soaking wet, and feet hurting like hell. I ran into one of the guys years later at Walmart and I will never forget what he said to me.

"Hey, how are you?" I asked him.

"I'm good, how are you, what are you doing these days?" "I'm a mental health therapist."

"I always knew that you would do great things, it was nice seeing you!"

It was in that moment I realized that people saw things in me back then that I was unable to see for myself. It was also a confirmation that I deserved great things.

Soon, I started doing a paper route because I needed money to pay off my evictions and buy furniture. I had no idea how hard it would be to run a paper route, attend school, and work full time. It was freezing cold, and the snow was to my knees. I woke up at 2 am, made it to the newspaper factory and started to get my papers ready. Due to exhaustion, I was moving slow and barely making it through my route. After my first two weeks of working, I received a BILL for 42 bucks. The newspaper company had charged me for not delivering all my papers. I went to work that night and I quit in the middle of my paper route. I had done all that hard work for nothing. Thank God I only wasted two weeks on that hustle.

Jalil was spending more and more time at his people's house, so that's where I would drop Ladybug off to. One day, I was dropping Ladybug off and as I got out of the car, a family friend, Rachel, sucker punched me right in the mouth. I honestly can't remember much, but I do remember feeling fear. I had been in a fight before, but I no longer had anything to prove. I had a feeling that Jalil was sleeping with Rachael because she had started acting upset anytime I dropped off Ladybug. I didn't think much of it because Jalil said I was tripping. Instead of dropping off Ladybug, I jumped in my car, put my foot on the gas, and sped out of the parking lot. I didn't understand why Jalil continued to cheat on me. My life was pure chaos, and I knew something needed to change. I wanted better.

Jalil was also messing with another woman named Nia. I can't recall how I found out, but I do remember the pain. If you have ever been hurt by a man you love, then you know exactly this pain that I speak of. It's the ultimate hurt for any woman. He didn't have enough respect to wear a condom and he didn't hide her. I just showed up at his house and there she was.

Financially, I was struggling to keep up. Although I knew how to make money, saving it was not a thing. Getting to work became a burden because I could barely keep gas in my car, let alone insurance, but I had to do what I had to do to survive. One night, I was on my way home and ran out of gas. It has been a long day and I had worked and gone to school that day. Luckily, I was able to pull up to the gas station. One of Ladybug's cousins could sense that I was stuck.

"Hey, you, okay?" "Actually, I ran out of gas"

"Man, this is all I can give you right now," she said, reaching into her pocket and handing me a five-dollar bill.

Even though the weight of embarrassment was overwhelming, that moment motivated me to no end. Leaving the gas station that night, I made a promise to myself that I would never allow myself to have zero dollars in my pocket again. I was motivated to make sure that I never had another experience like that and I never have. That's power.

What took my power - Myself
Truth, I needed to accept - I was broken

When you are born into brokenness it can become a lifestyle. It takes work to pull yourself out of that. You must change your entire being. I was my biggest barrier. Inside, I was battling myself and it showed. I had given my power to everyone and everything that wasn't for me. I was feeding the wrong energy and blaming my mother and Omar for my life being so hard. I had to learn that no one could take my power unless I gave it to them. In this book, some of my most intimate moments are revealed; many of which I am not proud of. I am at a place in life where I have accepted every part of me. This means no one can use my story against me. I know I have short-comings and I embrace them. It takes a lot of self-reflection, self-forgiveness, and self-encouragement, but you know more than anybody who you truly are. I urge you to find yourself.

Tips on how to find yourself

Get into therapy: It took a while, but I finally realized that I could not heal on my own. I needed therapy. I was lost and needed help finding my way back to myself. I needed help figuring out who I was. You must find the right therapist and you must do the work outside of your sessions.

Understand yourself and your triggers: Every part of who I was, was rooted in my trauma. It was hard to accept this truth because it showed I had a lot of work to do. One biggest barrier was the way I defended myself when I felt someone was attacking me. I was unable back then to identify my triggers. I had to understand that if I didn't understand what was triggering me, I would never see them coming. I struggled in life, key word "I". This behavior impacted my job, and my relationships, and it made things harder for me. I have learned that a woman who walks in her power is a woman who knows how to be still and have peace. So every day, I try to become her. I remember being young and ignorant not caring how I showed up. Finally, I understood two things; first off, I was fighting unnecessary battles. I had been defending myself for so long that reacting and defending myself were embedded in who I was. Of course, we should defend ourselves, but only when it's truly necessary. I must wake up and remind myself that today, I have nothing to defend. Secondly, going through struggle after struggle made me build a brick wall and it also made me defensive. Think what you want and say what you want; I cannot feed myself this energy. Childhood trauma also causes you to be very defensive. It was hard for me to let go of everything that happened to me. I felt that I had the right to be angry. Of course, pain is powerful, but the things that hold power over you can only do so if you allow it. If you allow self-doubt to cripple you, it will do just that.

— 9 —

The Power of a Man

I slept for two whole weeks after finding out about Jalil getting another woman pregnant. I only got up because Ladybug had to eat, but now, I was tired of lying in bed. My baby was right next to me watching cartoons and sleeping off and on. It's hard to remember these moments because Ladybug deserved more. I cried until I could no longer cry anymore, and that's when I made a dramatic decision. It was the final straw. I moved out of my place and back in with my sister. I did not know it at the time, but we would never rekindle our relationship because once I got my power back, I walked away for good.

Deciding to move in with my sister was my only escape from him. He didn't know where I was, but I eventually called.

"Where the fuck is my daughter?" He still had no respect.

"She is right here." He didn't even ask to talk to her, he was more concerned about having control over me. I was done with him and so over it.

Once with my sister, I started a new job, and my plan was to never give Jalil another piece of me. I dropped Ladybug off at daycare and went to work. Although I missed Jalil and it hurt to be away from him, I knew I couldn't go back.

On my first day at my new job, I was already exchanging numbers with one of the supervisors. He was light-skinned, had green eyes, and was very handsome. His name was Brandon. You would think that after Jalil, I would have learned my lesson, but I was addicted to men. I could not function without having a man in my life, and

I hated being alone. The only time I truly felt whole was when I was with a man. I had no boundaries back then; in fact, I didn't even know what they were. No one had ever taught me the importance of healing after leaving an abusive relationship.

In no time, I was head over heels for Brandon. He gave me butterflies and I needed him. I bragged to my sister, and she told me that Brandon had a history of being abusive. I didn't believe her, I just thought she was jealous.

Brandon soon asked me to move in with him. He had his own place, no kids, and he appeared to come from a good home. I literally thought that he would be the man I would marry. I moved in with him along with Ladybug. In the beginning, everything was amazing. He cooked, cleaned, and worked. He was so different from Jalil and that made me pay less attention to the red flags. He was also very quiet which made it hard to figure him out. I will never forget stopping and praying when I first got with him. I told God that I did not want to have a child with another man who was not meant for me. Brandon and I tried for years to get pregnant, but my period came every month, and he would literally get upset when my period came. It got to the point of me hating my periods because I knew how he would react. I thought that God was punishing me for all the abortions I had in the past but, He was saving me.

While I was with Brandon, I dropped Ladybug off every Friday at her grandmother's house. It felt like Ladybug didn't fit quite as well in the familial relationship with Brandon, so I dropped her off as much as I could.

Brandon was an incredible lover. He was so affectionate, and I loved it. In the beginning, he smothered me with love, attention, and affection. Even though I felt this amount of love when I was with him, I could not be with someone who didn't love my child the way they claimed to love me.

One day while in the car, Brandon reached his arm in the back seat and grabbed Ladybug by her stomach. It pissed me off and I was already fighting some serious demons from my traumatic childhood. I loved Brandon, and honestly, if I didn't have Ladybug, I probably would have stayed with him. However, after the type of childhood I endured, there was no way I could live with myself if I allowed anyone to abuse my child. I was strong enough for her even when I couldn't be strong for myself. The look on Ladybug's face, when he did that to her, broke my whole heart. She was terrified. I was with Brandon for two years and that was another moment when I put Ladybug second. Brandon interacted with her when he was in a good mood, but if he was upset, he acted like she was not there. We would sit her in the room to watch TV and eat her snacks, but I would always have to keep a close eye on Brandon. He had issues far beyond what I had ever seen. Jalil was no good because he was a cheater, but Brandon was an abuser.

Brandon also blamed me for him losing his job. He felt that he had worked so hard to get that position and because I disclosed that we were together, they fired him (remember he was a supervisor). I felt fucked up because that was partially the truth. Luckily, Brandon had parents that were wealthy enough to help us pay our bills. His mother would bring us cooked meals and wash our clothes. Although grateful, I was still very uncomfortable with this kind of support because I never had it.

One night, while we were out at the bowling alley, Brandon suddenly had this evil look in his eyes,

"What's wrong?" I asked him, and then looked back at my sisters (who had recently moved back to Minnesota and were living with Omar's sister) to tell them that Brandon and I were going to the car to talk.

"What's wrong" I repeated myself, he looked angry, and I was confused as to why.

"I see you and your sisters in there laughing at me."

Brandon used to be a fat kid and he was teased a lot, so this showed up in his relationships. He was so insecure. I did not realize that I was entering the most dangerous relationship I would ever experience.

One night, months later, I was walking down the road as fast as I could with Ladybug tagging behind me trying to get away from Brandon who was in one of his random rages. I was holding Ladybug's hand, but she was still dragging behind.

"You better get back here," he yelled.

"No, come on Ladybug." It was at that moment that I heard a loud thump, it was Ladybug being hit by a speeding car. When I looked up, my baby's shoes were no longer on her feet, they were beside her limp body.

"What the fuck!" I screamed, "Call the ambulance." I picked her up and held her in my arms. "Ladybug, can you hear me?"

"Yes," she said, in her little cute voice.

Once we got home later that night, Brandon apologized repeatedly. Ladybug's dad showed up at the hospital with his family and they knew that Brandon was involved. They thought that he had ran her over with his car. I didn't feel safe telling them how she got hit by a car, so I just told them that she was hit by a car. I wish I could have told them that Brandon was chasing us down the street and that caused me to be negligent.

The next day, I came home from work to more craziness. There was so much shock at the shit I had allowed that at this point, I gave up the fight. I came home from work, and I did not know that Brandon's sister had emailed me through Facebook. As soon as I walked through the door, Brandon hit me in the face. I blacked out and when I woke up, I was lying in a tub filled with blood. I guess he put me in the tub to help me regain consciousness.

"Let me leave this house, now!" I yelled when I came to.

"I cannot let you do that," he was crying and shaking his head while looking at my face.

"What the fuck is wrong with my face?"

He just shook his head in disbelief. I jumped out of the tub, and it looked like someone had hit me in the face with a bag of rocks. My front tooth was also chipped. I begged him to let me leave. He held me captive for two weeks until my eye healed. He cooked and cleaned for me, and I slept most of those days. Not only was I depressed, I was once again suicidal.

I hadn't thought about Louis in so long, but during those two weeks, I did start to think about having him in my life again. Brandon grew more and more paranoid that I was cheating and so his anger turned into rage. As I curled up in my chair, while he stood over me with a lamp screaming and in rage, I could see it in his eyes that the wrong answer to this question could cost me my life.

"You got a call from a blocked number. I am going to ask you one more time, whose number is this?"

All I could do was hope he wouldn't bash my head in. I curled up bracing myself for the hit, then I heard his footsteps as he walked away.

Quickly, I jumped up and ran to the bedroom infuriated, but in fear, because I knew that he was stronger than me. Once I made it into the room, I did what I always did, I prayed. "God please, help me out of this situation, I am unable to get myself through this." I always talked to God because I have always felt Him, and at that moment, I needed him desperately because I felt completely powerless. There have been so many situations that I could never have made it through, without Him, and He has carried me. That was the last time I allowed any person to abuse me or stand in the way of my personal growth.

When you love a man, it's so easy to stay because love is strong. I was literally in prison in my own home, and he was the commanding officer. He had sex with me when he wanted to, spit in my face when I did not listen to his commands and made me feel like the most worthless person on earth. It's funny how life experiences give us better understandings and answers the questions we once had. I was disgusted with myself because I could not leave him. As a woman, that made me feel weak, and then crazy, because I could not figure out if I wanted to leave or stay with him. In those moments, I also often wondered if this was how my mom felt while being with Omar. I knew I wanted respect, but I had no idea how to get it from him. He was so mean to me.

"You hoe ass bitch." "What?"

"Bitch, I am not stupid, I know you are fucking around." "You're crazy!"

He started biting the side of my face until I cried for him to stop. I was so angry that I called my sister and told her that I was about to kill myself. In my mind, I knew I no longer wanted to be abused, but I had no idea how to leave because I had nowhere to go. It just made sense to choose death rather than to continue to allow someone who claimed to love me to continue abusing me. My sister called the police and before I knew it, I was in the back of a squad car headed to the Psychiatric unit on the 4th floor at Regions Hospital.

Talk about feeling like a crazy person. And to make matters worse, when they called my aunt for collateral, she told them that I had been through a lot and probably needed help. I was so tired of being blamed for my behavior. How much abuse was I supposed to take before I was "allowed" to breakdown? They placed me on a seventy-two-hour hold. I eventually gave in and got some rest.

Later, I was awakened by a nurse who was asking me for a urine specimen and to take some pills.

"I am not pissing or taking those pills," I combatted.

"Okay, but they will keep you here longer the more you resist," she shrugged.

I held my ground that entire day; many nurses were rejected.

In a panic, I woke up later to my door being wide open and an older black man walking back and forth in front of it. I jumped up in fear and ran right into the staff's office. They were all surprised by my behavior.

"You have to get out of this office." "That dude is scary as hell!"

"Oh, that's just Gary, he walks the halls every night."

Quickly, I decided to do whatever they said because I had to get up out of there. I provided urine the next day in hopes that I could go home sooner. Later that day, I had to be assessed by the psychiatrist as well. After everything I had been through, I was just now twenty-five-years old, and finally sitting in front of a professional.

"Hey, are you doing cocaine?" "Did I test positive for cocaine?"

"No, but you did test positive for Marijuana and usually people mix the two."

"First of all, I should not even be here. I am being abused and I am the one sitting in a psych ward! This world is fucked up. My whole life has been fucked up! You are coming in here with this white coat and you have no idea what I've been through! Imagine your stepfather trying to stick his dick in your mouth!"

She walked out of the room and her intern stood there crying. She looked at me and told me that it wasn't my fault. It felt as if a weight had been lifted and I felt so much lighter after saying that out loud. It was the first time I was ever able to say that out loud.

The following day, I was diagnosed with post-traumatic stress disorder. In anger and frustration, I told myself this was simply not true, and that white people were crazy. Brandon picked me up from the hospital, and once again catered to me. Once we made it home, I went straight to the bathroom, stood in front of the mirror, and decided I was finally ready to move forward. I bargained with God that if He would get me out of this situation, I would do better at choosing men.

Unfortunately, I did not leave right away and even when I did, I would come back.

"Girl, you aren't shit without me, your family doesn't love you and there isn't no way you're going to be able to pay rent on your own. Do you really think a street nigga like Louis is going to treat you good?" He asked, his eyes full of rage.

Hearing the way he spoke to me gave me flashbacks, and I could see Omar. It was weird. Brandon resented me for losing his job so much that he could not get an erection. We would be having sex and he would start thinking about everything he was going through and just lose touch and go limp. I would lie there frozen, wondering how I could escape him. Many times, I tried and tried, but I was not successful at escaping him; he had serious power over me.

One morning, I woke up and got ready to leave for work. I tried my best to act like things were normal. As I was about to head out the door, there was Brandon. He was sitting at the kitchen table smoking a cigarette and drinking a cup of coffee.

"Are you about to wash these dishes?" I could tell that he was upset, but I was irritated, and it was hard to keep my cool.

"I'm running late and it's only like two dishes, wash them."

He got up and grabbed me by my hair. He pulled me back to the sink. He forced me to wash the dishes that day. He had taken so much of me. I can't describe how powerless I felt. I tried to run out of the house, but of course, he caught me. He dragged me back into the house screaming and kicking. I didn't want to stay there, so I tried to calm him down.

"I'm sorry Brandon, can I please go to work?"

"All you had to do was wash the dishes, I won't be trying to out my hands on you," he attempted to reason.

He got his shoes on to drop me off at work. As soon as we got in the car, he realized that he had left his cell phone upstairs.

"Fuck, I left my phone upstairs. I'll be right back."

He left me in the car and my heart started beating fast, I was finally ready to leave behind that life, no matter what it took. I jumped in the driver's seat, and I pulled off ready for the consequence. He did everything he could to break me down and make me come back to him. He harassed me at work, he came to Ladybug's school, and he broke into my car. He made it clear that I was nothing without him. However, that time, I didn't go back.

I was so proud of myself, and still to this day, I haven't looked back. It was in that moment that something shifted in me. I started taking my power back, and more importantly, I believed that I could.

When I left Brandon, he did everything in his power to get me back. He called my internship site and told them that I was strung out on drugs. Although I was clearly dealing with chaos and not drugs, I received an email later that day asking if I could come to speak with the director. My heart was racing, and I knew that I was about to be fired from my internship site. I ran to my car and rushed to the administration building. Once in Jackie's office, she told me about the email she has received. She also gave me a poem. The poem was called, *There's a Hole in my Sidewalk"* by Portia Nelson.

> I walk down the street.
> There is a deep hole in the sidewalk.
> I fall in. I am lost.
> I am helpless. It isn't my fault.
> It takes forever to find a way out.
> I walk down the street.
> There is a deep hole in the sidewalk.
> I pretend that I do not see it. I fall in again.
> I can't believe I am in the same place.
> But it isn't my fault.
> It still takes a long time to get out. There is a deep hole in the sidewalk.
> I see it is there.
> I still fall in... It's a habit...but my eyes are open.
> I know where I am.

It is my fault.

I get out immediately.

I walk down the same street.

There is a deep hole in the sidewalk.

I walk around it.

I walk down another street.

For the first time in my life, someone believed in me and cared about me; at least that's what it felt like. She did not ask me for a drug test, she simply said, I understand and gave me the poem. I walked away feeling powerful. I was so upset with Brandon that once Louis was released from prison, I felt like he could heal me and make me feel better. After Brandon assaulted me, I looked up Louis on Facebook and he had posted his phone number. I called him.

"Hey," I said low and scared to speak. "Who is this?"

"Take a guess."

He paused, "I know this voice from anywhere, this is Sumiko!"

We both laughed. He asked to see me, and I gave him permission to see me at my job. He pulled up right away. He looked different. He was buff and he had on glasses. His skin was clear, but he had the same smile. He hugged me and I broke down crying because I needed that hug so much. I was over Brandon abusing me.

"Why are you crying? I mean, I knew you would be happy to see me, but man, I wasn't expecting you to cry." He laughed.

"No, it's not that. I'm afraid for my life right now." I confessed. "What! Oh, hell no! You do not have to go back home, it's that weird ass dude Brandon huh?"

"Yeah, like he is so crazy it scares me." "You need to leave. Why don't you?"

"I can't. I gotta get back to work. It was so nice seeing you though. I have your number and I will call you when I can."

After I left, I went to my sister's house, but again, I couldn't stay there long. This was the same sister who had put me and Ladybug out on the streets multiple times. I spent nights between her house and Louis' house. I tried to remain focused on school and my internship because my success was my only hope. I allowed Ladybug to stay at her grandmother's house when I stayed with Louis. I remember leaving for work one day and Jalil's uncle was outside. He was disgusting to me. He was one of those uncles that liked little girls. He was standing outside drinking a beer.

"Homeless Bitch," he spewed before taking a long swig of his beer. I sat in my car and processed those words. I can admit they hurt like hell because it felt like that was my truth. I was twenty-five years old practically living out of my car. I was a homeless bitch. Although I wanted to be better, daily, there were people, places and things that had power over me in a negative way. I went on with my day, but it was those things that made me go back to Brandon.

One day, he spat in my face and told me that if I did not get an abortion, he would kill me and himself and I believed him. When you're upset prior to getting an abortion, legally, they are supposed to send you home. The doctor told me that she would be sending me home, but I begged her to proceed, and she did. I was 4 ½ months pregnant, so they had to give me medication that would terminate the pregnancy, and then I would come back to have the pregnancy removed. I walked out of the office so numb; I didn't have any feelings inside. Brandon cooked for me and catered to me the entire night. I knew that once he allowed me to leave, I would never look back. Deep down, I knew that if he would hold me hostage and force me to kill a child, then he wouldn't hesitate to act on killing me. I lay in the bathtub as it filled with blood, I was miscarrying. The pain and agony shout through my body as I screamed from the pain.

The next morning, I woke up and headed back to the clinic. Brandon allowed me to go alone because he knew that the baby was no longer alive. That was the final straw, I never went back. He had taken so much life from me that I was willing to die to be free if that's what it was going to take. I was still standing and no matter how hard he tried, he couldn't stop me. He broke into my new car, hacked my Facebook, and showed up at my daughter's school threatening to kill her. He told me that I would never make it without him. He told me that my own mother didn't love me and that I was unlovable. No matter what he did to break me down, I stood tall, and I never went back.

What took my Power - A Man
Truth, I needed to accept - I did not know how to identify healthy love

As much as I hated my mother for allowing Omar to abuse her, I became a woman who allowed a man to abuse me, and I hated myself for it. I had to realize that I wasn't my mother. Eventually, I left that toxic relationship and I started to work on that part of me. It was during that time that I was introduced to the term codependency, and I had to accept that this was one of my issues. I was a woman who needed a man, instead of wanting a man. When it came to my life, I put men first and I allowed men to use me repeatedly.

This is a book about my truth, and I can be honest that this is still an area of growth for me. I am finally in a place of understanding this part of myself. I want to share some signs of codependency. The ones that I see a lot of women struggling with are:

- Lack of self-esteem/self-worth
- People pleasing
- Lack of boundaries
- In relationship after relationship
- Caretaking
- Unable to identify healthy love
- Feeling like you can't live without this person

If you are struggling with any of these signs, I would encourage you to explore this part of yourself.

Tips on how to let go of toxic love

Love yourself more: It's true what they say, "When a woman's fed up there isn't nothing you can do about it." The problem with this is that us women are strong as hell, which allows us to bear a lot. I pray that every woman will always put herself first and love herself more.

Let go of shame: If you're anything like me, I made the mistake of saying that I would never allow a man to put his hands on me. I was so ashamed of myself for allowing this kind of behavior that I hid it. The thing about domestic violence is that everyone around you knows what's going on, so really, you're only hiding it from yourself. You work through shame by showing yourself compassion.

Don't give his words power: Aside from physical abuse, verbal abuse is just as damaging. In my case, when the physical stopped working, he tried to verbally tear me down. He told me that I was unlovable and not good enough for him. He told me that no one would ever love me. He threw my past in my face and tried to use that against me. If I gave those words power, they would have destroyed me. Do not give other people's words power over your life, affirm yourself daily.

Heal before you date again: I can't tell you how important this tip is. Most women leave one abusive relationship only to find themselves in another. You must give yourself space to heal, and the best way to do that is through time. Get comfortable with being alone and learning to love yourself; especially if you struggle with codependency. You must have boundaries and vet properly before getting into a new relationship.

—10—

Breakthrough

At an early age, I was introduced to adversity, and every experience made me feel less powerful. It wasn't until I was able to change my mindset that I was able to embrace adversity. Never had I imagined that one day, I would wake up to a new perspective and start to understand why I was who I was. It was my internship site that helped me begin my healing process.

We were all meeting in the conference room for a team-building exercise. I did not know how powerful that day would be, but hindsight is 20/20. We were instructed to write a letter to a close friend and to date it with a later date, five years to be exact. In this letter, we were instructed to talk about things we hoped for. Writing this letter was easy, and exciting, then she asked us to come up in front of the group and read it out loud. My letter was written to AJ.

Dear Allen,

I hope all is well. I am writing you this letter to tell you how well I have been doing. I have finally finished school and received my master's degree. Ladybug is doing well, and my mom is five months sober. I paused because I could feel my eyes filling with water and my voice started to shake. The room got quiet, and I just stood there. I took a deep breath and finished reading.

I just finished writing my book and I can't wait for you to read it.

I will write again soon.

Sumiko

I sat down confused about what just happened. Why was that letter so hard to read? This was the first time I realized that I was still holding on to a lot of things that were weighing me down. The mere mention of my mom could still break me down in tears, and I had to admit that to myself. I thought I was good, or at least I tried to be, but trying to hold on to that kind of pain was destroying me inside. Immediately after work, I got on my knees and prayed. I asked God to soften my heart so I could forgive my mom and Omar. It was past time, and I was ready to let it go. I was tired of being angry.

The challenge had done so much for me. I worked there for a total of four years before it was my time to move on. As much as I enjoyed working in the company I know God positioned me for, some things started to bother me. I started to understand my role as a black woman in corporate America, and prior to working in corporate America, I never realized this was a thing. There were moments when I was faced with blatant racism and microaggressions. I chose this field believing that everyone had a pure heart and wanted to help people.

Originally, I was hired by a black woman named Mandy. Mandy was a force to be reckoned with. She lived in her truth and walked in her power. She was African, but she knew how to move in corporate America. When she left the company, something in me left with her and things changed for me, and eventually, I left The Challenge.

The morning after, I woke up and it felt like my back was against the wall. It felt like I couldn't show up, but deep down, I knew I had to. I knew that if I didn't show up, no one else would. I got out of bed, showered, and took a few minutes to reflect. Sitting down on the floor of the shower, I curled up and allowed the water to hit me. During that time of reflection, I reminded myself that I must own my part. If I continued to stress about things, I could not control, I was going to damage myself.

As a kid, I really couldn't prevent stress, but I could no longer use that excuse because I knew better. I knew the truth about chronic stress. I had reached a point in my life where I can no longer tolerate or allow stress to own me. My entire life had been lived on a battlefield surrounded by stress. My stress was about work, home life, my kids' progress, and believe me, I could go on and on. Although chronic stress is known, it's not highlighted enough. As a black woman, I already have so many risk factors that decrease my life expectancy, and stress is one of the main things.

If I never went to college, I wouldn't have even realized that as a black woman, statistics say I will not live a long life. I must wonder why something so important is hidden. A lot of us are asleep and we need to wake the hell up. If we continue to allow stress to own us, then it will do exactly what it's supposed to do, and that's kill us. Chronic stress almost broke me until I realized that I also had the ability to cope with it.

After leaving The Challenge, I decided to work for another big company. They had facilities all over town and they offered me a higher pay rate. It was a large facility for women struggling with addiction and mental health issues. We had sixty-four beds, and this program was not religious at all. In fact, it was the opposite of The Challenge. There was no chapel and there was no God. I was amongst staff of all white women, but I was used to that awkward feeling of being the only one. I was the only African American counselor on the clinical team and in most of my college classes. My co-workers would walk right past me as if I was invisible. Trust me, I felt it!

"Hey Holly," I said with a smile, I was always making them uncomfortable by speaking.

"Hey, Sam."

We met every morning for a flash clinical meeting. We went over every client and discussed how they did throughout the night.

"Um, Sha-tarious?" The woman struggled.

"Just call her Sha," another woman said, with a chuckle.

They all laughed, but I didn't find it funny, I thought that we should have strived to pronounce these kinds of names properly. I allowed them to call me Sam because they struggled to say Sumiko. Seriously, I wanted to know why they just couldn't get our names right? Was it that hard? Did they not realize that this was why I went by the name Sam? Simply working in corporate America is triggering for me as a black woman. I knew I had to get out of corporate America completely. With my mental health, it was not a good fit. I needed to be in healthy spaces to grow and this was not it. I felt like they had so much power over me. I couldn't just walk out and quit, or could I? How would I pay my rent? How would I finish my internship hours? The better part of me was able to push through.

Although I had been in the field for four years at this time, I was still being paid only $20 dollars an hour and my white colleagues with less experience were being put in higher positions. I won't lie, being treated like this empowered me to want more for myself. There I was with a bachelor's degree and years of experience but wasn't even being considered for a higher position. Starting my own treatment facility was becoming more and more of a real thing instead of me just thinking about it. No longer was I okay with staying in one position for the rest of my life. I knew I wouldn't be happy.

I started working on my business plan and I no longer cared about working hard at my 9-5 anymore. Work had me resentful and I longed to end my days before they even began. I started slacking on my paperwork and my attitude wasn't the best when I showed up to clinical meetings. Almost daily, someone would say something to piss me off. However, I tried my best to control myself because I didn't want to give in to the stereotype of being a mad black woman. I remember my supervisor would always assume that I was a single mom, and let's be real, that was because, in her mind, black women had children with men who didn't stick around.

"I understand what it's like being a single mom."

I just listened because who the hell told this woman I was a single mom? My kids were at home with their father at that very moment. It was just another thing that white women assumed about black women.

I started to feel fed up and silenced. Eventually, I started speaking up, and of course, I made every white woman cry. It's funny how they cry after they have offended someone. I noticed that black clients were being discharged at a much higher rate than white clients, so I brought it up to my superior.

She responded, "Oh wow, we can look at this, I will contact HR today and have them pull the numbers."

I waited several weeks, and they finally pulled the number. It turns out that I was right. The next day we had a training on diversity, that was the box that they checked to fix this problem.

Realizing this frustrated to no end because black people had to face systemic racism even in treatment facilities. I thought this was a safe space since we were there to help people get better. I was coming down the hall and there was Tonya, one of my co-workers, rushing by me. I could tell she was upset.

"Hey, what's going on?"

"They just fired me!"

"O wow, for what?"

"They say I had too many grievances too soon," she stated and ran out of the front door.

I immediately ran to find Alice.

"Alice, really?" I asked, flabbergasted by what I'd been told about Tonya.

"Really what?

"You guys know damn well those clients were coerced to file those grievances against Tonya."

Alice shrugged, "The team will be much better without her."

I just stood there in complete shock at the realization that no one is truly stable or safe in corporate America.

Walking out of the office that day, I was pissed, but also inspired. It was in that moment that I decided, without a doubt, that I was leaving corporate America to start my own treatment center. I was determined to give black people a safe space to receive treatment.

That night, I spent hours thinking about my future and how I was going to make myself better. I told myself that I wasn't going back. My internship was done, and I had some money saved up. Names for my treatment center started flooding my mind and I quickly found pen and paper to jot them down. I wanted to think of a name that had meaning. After thinking of a few, Breakthrough stood out to me. It was the perfect fit for my vision. That was the birth of Breakthrough Wellness Center.

Panic overtook me when the realization of me quitting my job set in. Although I had money saved up and I was eligible for unemployment (which was a lot due to the extra money that was being provided due to the pandemic), I was still overwhelmed with fear. I reached out to an old friend, Catie, to consult about how I would start my own treatment center. We met and she told me everything I would need to get started. I had to become licensed which was hard because I had to create policies and procedures. However, Catie was a lifesaver and provided me with a template.

Finally, I got my business license next and then I started working on my website and brochures. Then, I also started to accumulate office furniture. In my first license review, I thought I would only have a few things to fix but I had over forty items to fix. On June 15th, 2020, in the middle of a pandemic, I successfully opened my own treatment facility. Although I knew I needed to add a sober house, my credit was horrible and I didn't have any investors. However, I still moved forward.

What took my power - Lack of confidence
How I got it back - I never gave up and I believed in myself

Although I have had moments of attempting to take my life, I am still here. I have had moments when I have thrown in the towel, but I always got back up. This personal journey requires me to keep going no matter what. Even if I haven't faced my toughest battles, I am prepared for them. I know now that I can come back from anything if I allow myself to. Always remember that giving up takes away the chance of things getting better. Therefore, I urge you to keep going because I believe in you!

Tips on how to manage stress and have confidence

Practice patience and find strategies to problem-solve: We live in a world that moves fast. It tells us when we should have kids, when we should be married, and when we should complete college. I would encourage you to be the blueprint of your life and do what works for you. If you try to keep up with societal norms, you're going to feel exhausted. Find strategies that make your life work for you in your own time.

Practice meditation and spirituality: These days, I crave meditation and time to reflect. If you don't like to meditate, try it in small doses. It took me some time before I could meditate, so it may be the same for you. Try soothing yourself by listening to worship music. Of course, resting is good, but it can be hard to get rest when your mind refuses to turn off. You must try to shut down the noise; otherwise, you are resting in your stress.

Make a gratitude list: It is easy to identify the bad and feel sorry for yourself. However, can you identify the good? Making a list of the things you do have and are grateful for, can really help you put things into perspective.

Remember to breathe: If you've been through a lot, you may notice that at times, you forget to breathe. Remember to breathe, Inhale the good shit and exhale the bullshit. Practice different breathing techniques so you can calm yourself during moments of uncertainty and panic.

Be gentle with yourself: Always speak life into yourself. Forgive yourself when you fall short and remember that you deserve self-compassion.

Keep standing: Never stand down against any obstacle because you have the power to overcome it.

—11—

You are Powerful

Admittedly, I was in a space of feeling powerless for a long time, I lived there. After being put down and shitted on so many times, a person almost has no other choice but to struggle to believe in oneself. When looking for ways to build my self-confidence, I discovered the term imposter syndrome. I had struggled with this feeling for most of my life, so hearing this term helped me understand that part of me. Imposter syndrome is when you doubt your abilities and feel like a fraud. It's hard to step into your power when you don't believe you deserve it. When you feel that power makes sense in the hands of someone else, but in your hands, you feel as though you're a thief or a fraud. Imposter syndrome is rooted in you not believing in yourself and feeling like you don't deserve more. I felt this most of my life, but I didn't have words for it. When I was introduced to the term imposter syndrome, it made it easier to accept that part of me; because clearly, I was not alone. I didn't have to hide this anymore; I could embrace this and take back my power in this area.

When I was opening my business and completing my master's degree, I felt like the biggest fraud. I was opening a business without any investors and grad school was getting much harder. I was working two jobs, plus completing my internship, and I was exhausted. As much as I was doing everything I needed to do to open my business and finish my degree, inside me, I was doubting myself. My journey was risky. Statistically, I wasn't supposed to make it this far.

According to my past, I should have been on drugs, welfare, or maybe even dead. If my business needed money to keep going, I didn't have anyone to help me financially. On top of that, my credit was bad. Anyone in business would have told me that this was a risky plan, but I went for it because I had nothing to lose, but everything to gain. On the inside and even with me telling myself that I could pull this off, I still felt like a fraud. In rooms filled with people of power, I would freeze up every time. There was a voice in my head telling me that I wasn't good enough to be in those rooms. Of course, my business struggles did not make me feel any better. I wasn't getting clients or a response from my community. I was paying rent for a suite that I wasn't earning any profit in. I remember sitting in my office and opening an email from my landlord.

Sam,

Wondering what's going on with rent, again? Rent is due on the 5th business day of the month.

We are wanting to cut our losses and find another tenant at this time. We are willing to let you out of the lease and we would prefer to do this amicably and out of mutual respect.

Universe Buildings would like to rent this space to someone that can pay the rent and we are no longer willing to negotiate the terms of working with you on when rent is paid. Please let me know your thoughts. I'd rather do this without going through a formal process. We still have the heat, taxes, and mortgage payment to keep current on and your situation continues to grow and prevent us from continuing to do that on a timely basis.

My heart dropped, and instead of doing what I do best which is problem-solve, I panicked, I started talking negative to myself and I was ready to give up. However, I got down on my knees and prayed.

God, I am so lost right now. I don't know if this is for me, or not. I don't need a sign, I need to hear the words that I should keep going, Amen. I decided to go home for the day. As I was walking out of my office, a middle-aged black woman was staring at me. I was already irritated so I rolled my eyes and got in my car. Today was just not the day. I was a discouraged black woman in full effect. As I was backing up, I looked out my rear-view mirror and there she was about to get hit. I beeped my horn and backed out. She stood looking at my window, so I finally asked, "Ma'am, can I help you?"

She looked me right in the eyes and said, "I have a message from God, He told me to tell you to keep going because you're almost there."

"Thank you so much," was all I could say.

I drove home wondering if I was hallucinating because I never had a prayer answered that fast. For the first time in my life, I was fearful of God. I immediately emailed my landlord with a payment plan and from that day forward, I was able to manage paying for my suite. My clientele also began growing. You would think that I would have felt more confident, but the more successful I became, the more I struggled to feel like it was real.

Multiple things were happening at once that contributed to my imposter syndrome. My son was in the first grade, and he was unable to read, which made me feel like I was not a good mother. I was having issues at work with my coworkers telling me about my time management and calling me fat. My stomach was still hanging over my pants. I was still drinking Caribou coffee and eating tacos every Thursday.

One day, I decided that taking charge was key. Instead of me sitting in these negative thoughts, I continued to take charge. We came up with study time for my son. Continuously, I encouraged Ladybug to be better. I got my shit together at work and I began my fitness journey. I've always been my biggest critic and that's a good and bad thing. It holds me accountable, but it can also make me feel like shit. This is why balance is important. Operating a business requires exactly what they said it would. It required my time, my faith, and lots of hard work.

Now let's go back for a second. My imposter syndrome began long before I got my master's degree and started my business. When I enrolled in community college, half of me believed that I could do it, but the other part was scared that I would fail. For years, I could hear

Brandon's words, "You won't be able to make it on your own," and a part of me believed him. I was a single mom, a battered woman, and I had no support. All odds were against me, but I went for it anyway. Enrolling back into school was empowering and it made me feel like I was positively contributing to the world. I wanted to become a therapist or a teacher growing up, so I took that path. I enrolled in the alcohol and drug counseling program at Century college to become an addiction counselor. Prior to college, I had never really considered this major; but I wanted to help families dealing with addiction, so this major made the most sense.

I will never forget my first year in college. I was so excited about class. It was nothing like high school because I wanted to learn now. Even though I was homeless and leaving an abusive relationship, my mindset had completely changed, and I was no longer the same Sam from high school.

Every class, without fail, I showed up and I did the work. I had some cool teachers too. I could tell that they had good in them. They taught in a way that was easy for me to understand. They also inspired me and made me believe in myself. I remember walking out of my first class feeling defeated. That critic inside told me that I was a client, not a counselor. I was the only black woman in most of my classes and that alone made me feel discouraged. After class, I waited for everyone to leave and approached my professor's desk to speak with her.

"Do you think I have what it takes to be a counselor?"

She looked at me, smiled, and said, "You were born to do this." I smiled back and went home feeling good.

She was a good professor, she gave me so much wisdom that is still with me today. Hope is what she said my clients needed most and she was positive I could give it to them. At that time, her statement left me feeling confused, but I shook my head as if I understood. Of course, I eventually understood what she meant. She basically meant that helping someone find hope in something greater helps them believe in possibility and hopefully, they are moved enough to get up and take control of their lives. I will never forget her. Her name was Debra, and it was her words that made me believe in my abilities and gave me confidence.

Prior to being in her class, I was a prisoner of my insecurities, but her words freed me for a moment. I needed reassurance because I didn't feel adequate. So many people had told me that I was nothing and deep down, I believed that. Coming from poverty and people with low levels of education made me question my audacity to even seek something higher. I was a high school dropout. How was I going to make it through college?

Negative self-image and negative thoughts will keep you stuck. It took me most of my life to find my confidence and at times, I still feel inadequate. However, I have learned to realize that I didn't have to act on negative feelings.

Attending college and sitting in those classes made me feel powerful. Knowing I wanted nothing more than to graduate made it easy to keep going. I owed that to myself. Every day, I showed up for myself, even when I didn't feel like it. On days when I felt depressed, and when I felt like giving up, I got up. I watched my progress through the student portal like a hawk, and every time I completed a semester, I was overjoyed because it meant I was closer to fulfilling my dream of becoming a college graduate. My grades were amazing all through school. However, during my last semester, my GPA dropped tremendously to 2.6. I had taken a math and science class that almost took me out of graduation completely. Those were the areas I'd always struggled the most in. The other classes came easy for me, but math and science were like foreign languages.

I studied my ass off and I ended up passing both classes with a C average. It was a lot, but for the first time in my life, I had completed something great! Graduating from a community college is nothing for some people, but it was everything for me. I stood there in my cap and gown reaping the benefits of my work. Only I'd known what it took to get here. I was sad that my mom was not there, and I was disappointed that I did not walk across the stage with honors. That darn negative critic in my head never failed to remind me of every shortcoming.

As I walked across the stage, tears drenched my face. I looked in the audience and there were a few of my siblings, my nephews, and Ladybug. It felt so good to walk across that stage. I was doing everything I said I would and that was a powerful moment for me. Making it through college proved something great for me. It proved that I was an overcomer, and I could do anything I set my mind to do when I refuse to give up. I attended every class. I owned it.

Yes, I still had really bad habits like, turning in assignments at the last minute and not reading as much as I should, but I did it. I was feeling so good that I immediately applied to Metropolitan State University to start working on my bachelor's degree; there was a fire that had been ignited in me, and I now had a list of things that I wanted to achieve. I told myself that I would not stop until I did everything on my list.

The List
- Bachelor's degree
- Master's degree
- Improve as a mother
- Lose weight
- Start my own treatment center
- Write a tips and tools book
- Build my house
- Get into public speaking
- Create generational wealth
- Have Peace

Why is this important? It's important because it's my proof to you that you can have everything on YOUR list. It is going to take massive action! However, it's possible. I remember telling my coworkers that I was going to write a book and open my own treatment center. Some of them told me I could do it and some of them thought I was crazy. Some of them even thought that I was grandiose. As I was going through the process of trying to make it through this list, I struggled. I had days when I questioned my own power: Maybe people are right, maybe this successful person who broke generational cycles wasn't me? I questioned myself a lot. I was still engaging in things that did not serve me, and making life harder for myself. I'd even gotten into, yet again, another relationship that was tearing me down. And believe it, or not, it was Louis. My first year at Metro State was hard as hell and I wanted to give up. I was being cheated on and abused. Louis was acting out, and I was finally about to become a mother for the second time. I went to school until the day I gave birth. I worked full time during the day and went to school at night.

On August 9, 2014, I gave birth to a son and named him Louis the third. His father was cheating on me, and I was struggling with depression because of it, which caused me to feel powerless. I went to school and work, but outside of that, I spent most of my time sleeping. Waking up every day, working, and going to school was draining. However, I knew I had come too far to give up. That negative voice in my head was loud and clear saying, "You just can't get your shit together."

I didn't understand why I allowed this kind of behavior. It frustrated me and made me hate myself. I did everything I could to hang on, and before I knew it, there I was walking across the stage for my bachelor's degree. No longer was I allowing the negativity in my life to have power over me, so I decided to keep going. One negative thought, or situation, can destroy your entire world and make you give up. Don't listen to that negative voice.

There was one class that made me feel like a failure and almost made me give up. It was a senior seminar, and it was run by two of the strictest teachers. I completed and turned in every assignment and still failed the class. I was livid. My anger was so powerful in that moment that I almost quit school. I went to speak to the dean of the school who told me that those teachers have been with the college for years and that I would lose a case against them. I walked out of there and accepted the truth. I had just wasted my time and had to retake this class. This moment became even more triggering because I had also run out of financial aid. I had to pay $5,000 to graduate or postpone my graduation.

As you already know, I was panicking and flipping out. I was thinking that everything was for nothing. Instead of thinking of a solution, I went straight to panic mode. It gets harder to walk in power if you have no faith. Yes, I was getting better, but it was an ongoing process. Every year, I gained new insight and did my best to implement changes. However, when life sucker punched me, it always took me a little while to bounce back.

This time, I swallowed my pride and borrowed the money from my younger sister. I paid her back as fast as I could. I also passed the senior seminar with an A the second time! I had walked across the stage again, but this time for my bachelor's degree. I was proud and I felt powerful. My sisters had brought my mom to that graduation and honestly, unlike my graduation from community college, I didn't want her there, I felt like it was too late. She had missed so many moments and I was still hurt about that. However, I made the most out of my special day anyway.

The year 2020 turned out to be one of the most challenging years in U.S. history, and for me personally. A pandemic hit and challenged the world in ways no one saw coming. I had big plans for 2020. I was supposed to graduate with my master's, start my own treatment center, and leave corporate America. It was also the year that I was supposed to finish my book. Looking back, it's funny because the world was about to hand me some challenges that I had never seen coming. I thought that for once, things were about to go the way I planned them.

Everything was going as planned. I celebrated the new year and was excited to finish up grad school and start my own treatment center. I knew that I could only afford to pay about $1,000 a month, and I found a space for $995 dollars, so I knew it was the space for me. I called up the leasing agent and was on my way to see the space.

"Hey, I'm Sam."

"I'm Tory, what kind of business are you starting?" "I'm starting a treatment center," I smiled.

"Okay, are you going to be able to pay the rent every month? "

"I can pay you three months' rent upfront to show you how serious I am."

"Okay, well, come in on the first of the month and we can sign the lease."

A smile spread across my face as we shook hands. That was the breakthrough I needed, and we now had a home. It was a small space, but it would work. It had one group room, one office, and a reception area. The maroon carpets and yellowish walls bugged me to no end. I asked the man if he could change the carpet, but he didn't want to do all that. It was okay for now. Honestly, I was so happy I could make anything work.

Even having everything I needed. struggling with imposter syndrome made it hard to believe that I could have a successful treatment center. You must figure out a way to keep going even when things happen outside of your control, that's how you walk in power. In April 2020, I woke up to a pandemic and a race war, and yet, I still felt empowered. The Corona virus had just hit the United States. I remember thinking that this would blow over soon, but years later, we are still in the thick of it. On top of the pandemic and things shutting down, I contracted the virus and had to quit both of my jobs. I collected unemployment and worked towards building my business.

One morning, I woke up to Louis putting his iPhone in my face. "Oh, my God! The police just killed a man on live." He was in shock.

Looking over in complete horror, I watched the murder of George Floyd. He was being murdered in front of the entire world in the city

I lived in. I turned my head away from the video, but I could still hear bystanders pleading with the police to let him up. Sadly, I thought to myself what's the big deal, just another black man killed by the police, we will never get justice. Little did I know that this death would make history and provoke change. It was right in my neighborhood where a man known as George Floyd was murdered by police. It's a deep-rooted pain watching someone continue to kill your people and you can't do a damn thing about it. It makes us feel powerless. They kill us and then look us right in the eyes and tell us that racism does not exist, then they call us thugs for looting and for protesting. In my mind, it's a lose/lose situation.

It's one of those things that literally hurts my heart and evokes fear within me. My brother, Tony, was murdered by the police. Having a black son worries me because I know that he could also be killed by the police. I know that he will be judged by his skin color. It was also one of those things I had to accept, or it would take my power. With all these things going on, I stood tall and continued to work on myself.

I completed my master's degree to become a mental health therapist, and then I founded my company Breakthrough Wellness Center to help adults and African American youth overcome substance abuse and mental health issues. I got blessed with two sober homes. My sister bought one and a friend of mine bought the other because they believed in my vision. By walking in my power, making declarations in my life, and owning my truth, I manifested my life into the life I desired. To this day, I get chills when I think about my ability to command the rooms in which I walk today. My new way of thinking is "no one or nothing can take my power". Not a job, not a man, not a bad day, nothing! I accept everything as it comes, and I live for me. There is so much power in letting go and allowing God to do His work. There is also power in living for you. As I continue my own personal journey, I want this book to always be a reminder to myself that I can do anything. On the days when I feel like a terrible therapist, I want this book to be a reminder that it's my truth, and my ability to have empathy for others, that honestly sets me apart from other therapists. Never will I pretend to be perfect, and I won't tell you how to live your life, but I will provide a safe space and allow you to heal authentically.

In my years of living, I had to learn that no one can take my power unless I give it to them. I revealed some of my most intimate moments in life; some that I am not proud of. I am at a place in life where I have accepted every part of me, so no one can use my story against me. It takes a lot of self-reflection, self-forgiveness, and self-encouragement, but you know more than anybody the obstacles you have overcame. I made a promise to God that if He allowed me to break through, then I would share my testimony to help others do the same. I am hoping that after reading this book, you will do one of two things, "take your power back, or never give it away again." I want you to know, right now, at this moment, that you are POWERFUL!

What took my Power - Imposter syndrome
How I got my power back - I claimed authority over my life

Now that you have made it to the end of the book, I will conclude my point. I took my power back when I accepted my truth; the good, the bad, and the ugly. There will always be adversity and sometimes I will fall short. We must accept the good with the bad and allow ourselves to experience it all. Suffering is a part of the human experience, so I embrace my struggles. Some of us will suffer more than others and that simply means you're a warrior. As humans, we have the power to overcome grief, pain, and feelings of inferiority. I have learned that the more you can learn to accept the bad things, the less you will be bothered by them. As I look back, it was my lack of self-acceptance, and confidence that held me back from owning my power. My battle was internal, and it took me a while to realize it, which caused me to remain stuck for years. Inside, I was battling myself and it showed. Unknowingly, I had given my power to everything and everyone. What also took my power was refusing to accept my past, this coincidentally caused me to reject my reality.

Therefore, acceptance is key when walking in power because it makes you better. Finally, I took charge of every area of my life. I took charge of my finances, my spiritual, my physical, my mental, my anger, and ultimately my happiness. And today, I refuse to stand down.

Three practical ways to cope with imposter syndrome

Keep Moving: Even if you're not the person you want to be, keep moving towards that image of yourself until you get there.

Self-compassion: If you're having a hard time believing in yourself, practice more self-compassion. No matter what, even if you do not believe it, keep telling yourself that you do. If you struggle with that, write it somewhere, buy a candle, a poster, or something that can remind you of how powerful you are.

Look at the facts. Write down your wins. How many times have you failed and how many times have you gotten back up? If you are still standing, that is proof that you can get back up.

Do not engage with people who make you question yourself; they will keep you feeling like a fraud.

Tips on how to walk in your power

Own your truth: Owning your truth is a must if you want to walk in power. You must own your story to the point that no one can use it against you. You must own your mistakes and your shortcomings. People have tried to use my story against me many times, but today, I know who I am. I have admitted my mistakes, and I own my shortcomings. No one can use my past against me.

Celebrate your wins: A lot of us play small for whatever reason. If you did better today than you did yesterday, celebrate that. Celebrate every win and every milestone so you can remind yourself that you are important and capable of all things.

Let go of the things that were sent to destroy you: This is a big one! It's a complicated concept but we all hold on to things that we shouldn't. The problem comes in when we hold on to it for too long. It eats away at us causing us to lose power. People operate with their emotions and oftentimes the emotions are prevalent simply because of the weight they are carrying. This causes them to react immediately when they feel threatened in any way. You will have poor communication skills and damaged relationships if you don't know the difference between who and what is for you. Let it go!

Have faith: I was the queen of worry. If you're going to walk in power, then you must make sure that your faith is bigger than your fear.

Take Charge over your life: It was at the start of my career that things shifted for me. I finally felt something greater, and I was willing to work hard to keep it. No longer was I willing to give in to my moments of self-doubt or wanting to give up. To take charge is to take full control over everything in your life, and sometimes that includes letting go. This is a hard one, but if you can achieve it, you become unstoppable. If you want to lose weight, change your eating habits and exercise. If you want financial freedom, tell your job to boss up, or move on. Your possibilities become endless. I get it, sometimes we are in situations that we cannot control. I took charge of every aspect of my life, and it worked. Making better choices allowed me to feel a sense of peace within, knowing that I was the captain of my own ship. Only a small part of your life is what happens to you, the larger part is how you choose to respond to it.

Accept the things that you cannot change: The serenity prayer is not only for addicts but for anyone who has a hard time understanding what to hold on to and what to let go of. The prayer is as follows:

"God grant me the serenity to accept the things that I cannot change, the courage to change the things that I can and the wisdom to know the difference."

I always knew that one of my gifts was to help others, so after I picked myself up, I set out to do just that. I wanted to give back and change the things I could. I wasted years trying to change the things

I couldn't and when I finally accepted my past, I knew I could move on to something greater.

Stand in your truth: When you are stable and consistent with who you are, it makes you powerful. No one can break you or stop you. No one can challenge who you are because you're sure of yourself. The dreams will start to come true and everything you have worked for will be yours. You will be faced with your truth, and I urge you to stand in it.

Patience: It's easy to feel powerless when you don't have patience. In this life, you must understand that nothing happens just because we want it to. If you don't practice patience, you're going to be an irritable person or even worse, you might give up. Your failures cause you to feel hopeless and your ability to endure will be non-existent. You won't be able to accept problems or delays. I wanted this book written a long time ago, but I had to go through a ten-year process before this dream came true. There was delay after delay, problem after problem, but I had to decide to keep going.

You must decide to keep going, too. The closer you get to your dreams, the more you can feel them. A lot of the time, we give up when we can't feel things happening the way we want them to happen. During the process of me writing this book, it took me ten years due to my lack of patience. Having patience is the most powerful tool one can possess.

Don't believe the lies: There is only one truth and that's the truth as it relates to self. You're the only person who gets to determine who you are. Knowing, without a doubt, that I am a good person is why I can live with myself even if someone else perceives me as bad. There is no way I can live up to everyone's standards and I'm okay with that because most people don't truly know me. A wise professor once made this very profound statement to our class, "It should never be who we are but why we are?" You can know who you are but that's not good enough. You must know why you are who you are so that you can always live in your truth.

Reflection questions:

Are you okay with yourself? Why or why not?

_____
_____
_____
_____
_____

Do you know your truth? If so, what is it? If not, why do you think that is?

_____
_____
_____
_____
_____

Do you know why you are who you are? If so, who are you and what makes you, you? If not, what steps will you take to try to discover who you are?

_____
_____
_____
_____
_____

Can you identify ways in which I may have overlooked someone attempting to help me and what trauma may have caused me to overlook the help?

_____
_____
_____
_____
_____

In what ways have you overlooked someone trying to help you during a struggle? How will you approach accepting a helping hand or a way out in the future?

_____
_____
_____
_____
_____

Have you ever thought about seeking therapy for childhood traumas you may need to address and overcome? If you are seeing a therapist, is it helping you address and accept your childhood traumas?

_____
_____
_____
_____
_____

"Understand this, you are powerful! You have the power to win, to fight, to conquer, to thrive, to prosper, and to rise"

About the Author

Sam Knight is a force to be reckoned with. She is a woman of God, mother, business owner, breakthrough coach, addiction counselor, psychotherapist, motivational speaker, and now an author. Originally born, Sumiko Knight in Newburgh N.Y., Sam has lived most of her life in Saint Paul, MN where she currently resides. Not only has she had to overcome molestation and childhood trauma, but she has also battled with mental health issues, domestic violence, and many more obstacles.

In 2015, after realizing she had become powerless due to traumatic experiences in her life, she left her abusive fiancé wearing only the clothes on her back. She decided, in that moment, that she was going to fight for herself and take her power back.

In 2016, she received a Bachelor's degree in Addiction Counseling, and in 2020, she received a Master's degree in Clinical Mental Health Counseling. That same year, she also founded Breakthrough LLC.

Breakthrough is a substance use disorder treatment center, which to the glory of God became a six-figure business in 2022. With her story and success, she hopes to inspire others to take their power back, learn how to thrive in it, and never give it away again.

Acknowledgement

Thank You

Writing this book has been healing and challenging, in so many ways. I want to thank Reea Rodney at Dara's publishing for helping me finish this book. Finding the right publishing company is key when you need help finishing your book – especially if you're not a writer. I came into this process feeling defeated because of the things I could not change. I didn't see myself as a good writer, and I couldn't afford a ghostwriter, so my only option was to write this book myself. I started a long time ago, ten years to be exact. It wasn't until I was exposed to Dara's publishing that things really became serious, and I was able to get this book written. Reea, you have been a gift from God during this process.

I was procrastinating but you pushed me to keep going. You reached out to me, and you continued to encourage me to finish what I had started. You, cheering for me is proof that encouragement works, and yet it proves, even more, why I had to write this book to encourage others to walk in their power. Again, Reea, thank you! I would also like to acknowledge some very important people in my life because, without them, life would be harder. I want to thank my three children who have been my motivation throughout this process. Secondly, I would like to thank my life partner, Allen, for believing in me and being a great father to our children while I worked on my business and my book. I would like to thank my village, Gierra, Lanae, latoya and Desiree, you all have been by my side and encouraged me to write this book. Finally, I would like to acknowledge God because without Him none of this would be possible.